Surprisingly Simple
QUILTS

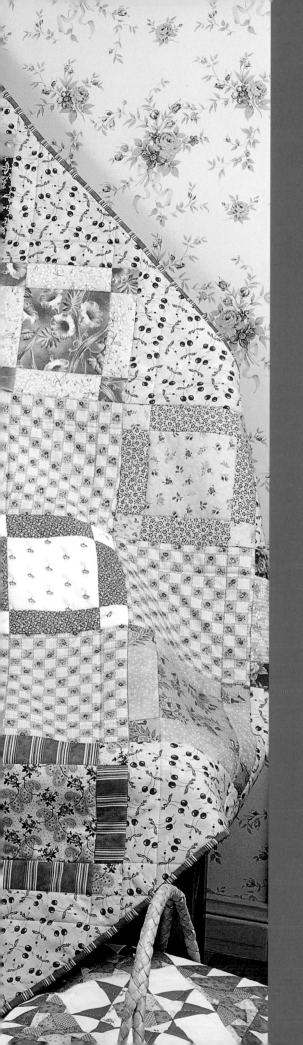

Surprisingly Simple QUILTS

From *Australian Patchwork & Quilting* Magazine

Martingale®
& C O M P A N Y

Surprisingly Simple Quilts
© 2006 by Martingale & Company

That Patchwork Place® is an imprint of
Martingale & Company®.

Martingale & Company
20205 144th Avenue NE
Woodinville, WA 98072-8478 USA
www.martingale-pub.com

Printed in China
11 10 09 08 07 06   8 7 6 5 4 3 2 1

Library of Congress Cataloging-in-Publication Data
Surprisingly simple quilts.
          p. cm.
     ISBN 1-56477-667-0
1. Patchwork—Patterns. 2. Quilting. 3. Patchwork quilts.
I. Martingale & Company.
     TT835.S8356 2006
     746.46'041—dc22
                              2005033913

Mission Statement
**Dedicated to providing quality products
and service to inspire creativity.**

Credits

President: Nancy J. Martin
CEO: Daniel J. Martin
VP and General Manager: Tom Wierzbicki
Publisher: Jane Hamada
Editorial Director: Mary V. Green
Managing Editor: Tina Cook
Technical Editor: Laurie Bevan
Copy Editor: Liz McGehee
Design Director: Stan Green
Illustrator: Laurel Strand
Cover Designer: Stan Green
Text Designer: Trina Craig
Photographer: Brent Kane

Contents

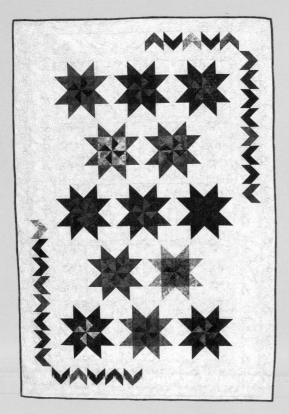

Introduction

Wouldn't it be wonderful to have days, weeks, or even months to simply quilt, quilt, quilt? Many quilters daydream about quilting cruises, weekend retreats, and the like—but life pulls us in all directions. Jobs, kids, meals, meetings, and more can take up so much of our day that we're left with only snippets of time to devote to quilting. The good news is that small stretches of time are all you'll need to start, finish, and enjoy the quilts in this book. This delightful pattern collection keeps the focus on simple yet stunning projects for giving—and for keeping!

In *Surprisingly Simple Quilts,* some of Australia's best and brightest designers have contributed clever ideas for quick-to-make quilts. Easy rotary-cutting, machine-piecing, appliqué, and embroidery techniques are featured in 13 charming projects. Most designs are based on trouble-free traditional blocks, such as Courthouse Steps, Pinwheel, and Puss in the Corner. All of the sewing methods, fabrics, and finishing options have been chosen to ensure smooth sailing on your next quilting adventure.

These medium-sized designs are perfect for quick gifts, wall hangings, table drapes, cuddly throws—even quilts for babies and kids. A variety of styles and colorways will inspire you to sew for yourself or for anyone on your gift list, year in and year out. New to quilting? No worries—a "Quiltmaking Basics" section will give you all the guidance you need!

So carve out a little time in your day—just a little!—to sit down, relax, and browse the inspiring projects in this book. Then take the precious time you *do* have to quilt and get started on one of these *Surprisingly Simple Quilts*!

Finished Block Size: 16" x 16" (41 cm x 41 cm)
Finished Quilt Size: 56½" x 88½" (144 cm x 225 cm)

Fairies in the Garden

Gorgeous fairy fabric was the inspiration for this delightful quilt by Kathy Doughty, but the quilt would be just as pretty made up in different fabrics. Any young lady would adore having this quilt for her bedroom. It's made with just two blocks, which are easy to construct using quick rotary cutting and machine-piecing techniques.

Materials

Amounts are based on 42"-wide (107 cm) fabric.

- ✦ 2¼ yards (2 m) of yellow-and-green striped fabric for Star blocks, Pinwheel blocks, and binding
- ✦ 1¾ yards (1.5 m) of multicolored striped fabric for Pinwheel blocks
- ✦ ¼ yard (20 cm) *each of 7 prints* for Star blocks and Pinwheel blocks
- ✦ 1½ yards (1.3 m) of fairy print for Star blocks and border
- ✦ ⅛ yard (10 cm) *each of 7 striped or checked* fabrics for Star blocks
- ✦ ¼ yard (20 cm) of yellow print for Star blocks
- ✦ 5 yards (4.5 m) of backing fabric
- ✦ 60" x 91" (150 cm x 230 cm) piece of batting

Cutting

All cutting dimensions include ¼" seam allowances. Instructions are for cutting strips across the fabric width unless otherwise specified.

From the yellow print, cut:
- ✦ 4 strips, 1½" x 42"; crosscut into:
  - · 7 pieces, 1½" x 6½"
  - · 14 pieces, 1½" x 5½"
  - · 7 pieces, 1½" x 4½"

From the fairy print, cut:
- ✦ 2 strips, 4½" x 42"; crosscut into 4 strips, 4½" x 18½"

From the remaining fairy print, cut *lengthwise:*
- ✦ 4 strips, 4½" x 38½"
- ✦ 9 squares, 4½" x 4½"

From *each of the 7 striped or checked* fabrics, cut:
- ✦ 1 strip, 1½" x 42"; crosscut into:
  - · 1 piece, 1½" x 8½"
  - · 2 pieces, 1½" x 7½"
  - · 1 piece, 1½" x 6½"

(Continued on page 12)

From the yellow-and-green striped fabric, cut:

✦ 4 strips, 8½" x 42"; crosscut into 28 rectangles, 4½" x 8½"

✦ 4 strips, 4½" x 42"; crosscut into 28 squares, 4½" x 4½"

✦ 8 strips, 2½" x 42"

✦ 5 squares, 4⅞" x 4⅞"

From *each* of the 7 prints, cut:

✦ 8 squares, 4½" x 4½" (56 squares total)

From 1 of the 7 prints, cut:

✦ 3 squares, 4⅞" x 4⅞"

From *each* of 2 of the 7 prints, cut:

✦ 1 square, 4⅞" x 4⅞" (2 squares total)

From the multicolored striped fabric, cut:

✦ 10 strips, 5½" x 42"; crosscut into:
  · 8 pieces, 5½" x 16½"
  · 16 pieces, 5½" x 11½"
  · 8 pieces, 5½" x 6½"

Making the Star Blocks

1. Sew a 4½"-long yellow print piece along the top of seven of the 4½" fairy-print squares; press each seam toward the yellow piece. Turn each unit 90° counterclockwise and sew a 5½"-long yellow print piece to the unit; press as before. Turn each unit 90° counterclockwise again and sew another 5½"-long yellow print piece to the unit; press. Turn each unit counterclockwise once more and sew a 6½"-long yellow print piece to the unit and press. The unit should measure 6½" square.

2. Add a second round to each unit as in step 1, using the striped or checked fabric pieces. The unit should now measure 8½" square.

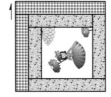
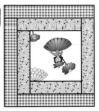
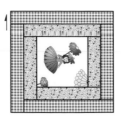

3. You will use four of the 4½" x 8½" yellow-and-green striped rectangles and eight 4½" print squares (all eight from the same print) to make flying-geese units for each Star block. Draw a diagonal line on the wrong side of each of the 4½" squares and draw a second line ½" away from the first line toward the corner. Place one square on one end of each 4½" x 8½" rectangle, right sides together as shown, and sew on both lines. Cut between the lines so that each piece has a ¼" seam allowance. Press both seams toward the print fabric. Set the half-square-triangle units aside for the Pinwheel blocks. Sew another square on the opposite end of each rectangle as shown; trim and press as before.

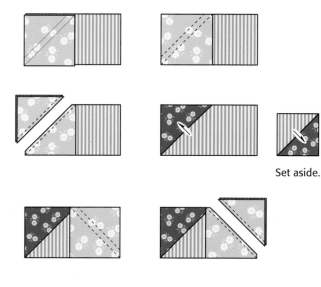

Set aside.

Make 4 of each point   Set aside.
(28 total).

4. Sew two of the matching flying-geese units to the opposite sides of a framed square as shown and press the seams toward the framed square. Sew a 4½" yellow-and-green striped square to each end of the remaining two matching flying-geese units; press the seams toward the striped squares. Sew these units to the top and bottom of the block as shown and press the seams toward the print points. The finished block should measure 16½" square.

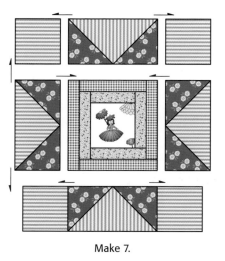

Make 7.

Making the Pinwheel Blocks

1. Using 32 of the half-square-triangle units (eight sets of four matching fabrics) from step **3** of "Making the Star Blocks," trim the units to 3½" square and be sure to align the 45°-angle line of your ruler with the seam line to ensure the seam is in the center. Place the trimmed squares in sets of four matching fabrics and sew them together as shown. Each unit should now measure 6½" square.

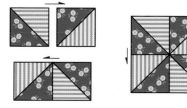

2. Sew a 6½"-long multicolored striped piece along the top of each of the pinwheel units; press the seam toward the multicolored piece. Turn the unit 90° counterclockwise and sew an 11½"-long multicolored striped piece to the unit; press as before. Turn the unit 90° counterclockwise again and sew another 11½"-long multicolored striped piece to the unit; press. Turn the unit counterclockwise once more and sew a 16½"-long multicolored striped piece to the unit and press. The finished block should measure 16½" square.

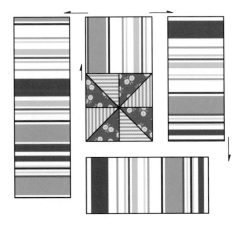

Assembling the Quilt-Top Center

Lay out the blocks in five rows of three blocks each, alternating the Pinwheel blocks and the Star blocks as shown. Sew the blocks together into rows and press the seams toward the Pinwheel

blocks. Sew the rows together and press the seams in either direction.

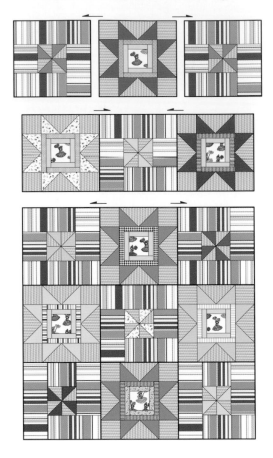

Adding the Border

1. Use the five 4⅞" yellow-and-green striped squares and the five 4⅞" print squares to make the half-square-triangle units for the border. Draw a diagonal line on the wrong side of the yellow-and-green striped squares. Place them right sides together with the print squares and sew ¼" from each side of the line. Cut along the line and press the seams toward the print triangles. You will have six half-square-triangle units of one print and two units each of two other prints.

2. Sew two of the six half-square-triangle units from a matching print between the four 38½"-long fairy-print strips as shown. Be sure the fairy print faces the correct direction. These are the side borders.

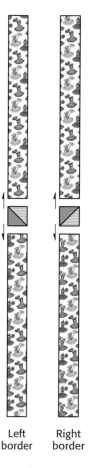

Left border   Right border

3. Sew the four remaining half-square-triangle units from a matching print to one end of the four 18½"-long fairy-print strips as shown. Be sure the fairy print faces the correct direction. Sew the remaining two pairs of half-square-triangle units from a matching print to each side of the two remaining 4½" fairy-print squares. Sew these two units between the 18½" fairy-print strips as shown. These are the top and bottom borders.

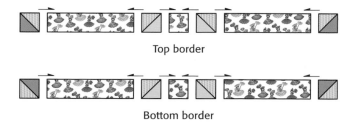

Top border

Bottom border

4. Sew the two side borders to the quilt-top center and press the seams toward the borders. Sew the top and bottom borders to the quilt-top center and press the seams toward the borders.

Finishing

Refer to "Preparing to Quilt" on page 91, "Quilting Techniques" on page 92, and "Finishing Techniques" on page 93 for detailed instructions if needed.

1. Make a backing that is 4" to 6" longer and wider than the quilt top. Cut the backing fabric into two equal lengths, remove the selvages, and sew the two pieces together along the length to make a backing with a vertical seam. Press the seam to one side. Mark the quilt top if necessary.

2. Layer the backing, batting, and quilt top, smoothing each layer from the center outward as you go. Baste the three layers together using your preferred method. Hand or machine quilt as desired.

3. Trim the batting and backing even with the edges of the quilt top. Add a hanging sleeve if desired. Using the eight 2½"-wide yellow-and-green striped strips, prepare the binding and sew it to the quilt. Make a label and attach it to your quilt.

Finished Quilt Size: 58½" x 58½" (150 cm x 150 cm)

The Dunsborough Quilt

Lee Bendtsen created this striking strip-pieced quilt in two colors. These quilts are traditionally red and white or blue and white; however, Lee's remarkable quilt stands out from the rest with a slight variation. Lee used dark pink and cream with a lighter pink inner border to highlight the central design.

Materials

Amounts are based on 42"-wide (107 cm) fabric.

- ◆ 2½ yards (2.3 m) of dark pink print for blocks, sashing, and inner and outer borders
- ◆ 1½ yards (1.3 m) of cream tone-on-tone print for blocks and sashing
- ◆ ½ yard (50 cm) of light pink print for middle border
- ◆ ⅝ yard (50 cm) of pink solid fabric for binding
- ◆ 3½ yards (3 m) of backing fabric
- ◆ 62" x 62" (160 cm x 160 cm) piece of batting

Cutting

All cutting dimensions include ¼" seam allowances. Instructions are for cutting strips across the fabric width.

From the dark pink print, cut:
- ◆ 10 strips, 4½" x 42"; crosscut 4 *strips* into 25 squares, 4½" x 4½"
- ◆ 23 strips, 1½" x 42"

From the cream tone-on-tone print, cut:
- ◆ 3 strips, 4½" x 42"; crosscut into 24 squares, 4½" x 4½"
- ◆ 18 strips, 1½" x 42"

From the light pink print, cut:
- ◆ 5 strips, 2½" x 42"

From the pink solid fabric, cut:
- ◆ 7 strips, 2½" x 42"

Making the Quilt-Top Center

1. Sew 18 of the 1½"-wide dark pink strips to the 1½"-wide cream strips in pairs lengthwise to make 18 strip sets. Press the seams toward the dark pink fabric. From 13 of the strip sets, cut 112 segments, 4½" wide. From the remaining 5 strip sets, cut 128 segments, 1½" wide.

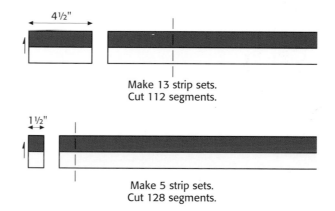

Make 13 strip sets.
Cut 112 segments.

Make 5 strip sets.
Cut 128 segments.

2. Sew pairs of the 1½"-wide segments together as shown to make 64 four-patch units.

Make 64.

3. Sew eight of the four-patch units and seven of the 4½"-wide strip-pieced units together as shown to make sashing row A. Be sure the colors are placed correctly. Press all of the seams toward the right. Repeat to make a total of four rows.

Sashing row A.
Make 4.

4. Sew eight of the four-patch units and seven of the 4½"-wide strip-pieced units together as shown to make sashing row B. Be sure the colors are placed correctly. Press all of the seams toward the right. Repeat to make a total of four rows.

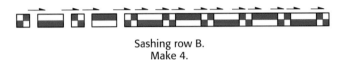

Sashing row B.
Make 4.

5. Sew four of the 4½" dark pink squares, three of the 4½" cream squares, and eight of the 4½"-wide strip-pieced units together as shown to make block row A. Be sure the colors are placed correctly. Press all of the seams toward the left. Repeat to make a total of four rows.

Block row A.
Make 4.

6. Sew four of the 4½" cream squares, three of the 4½" dark pink squares, and eight of the 4½"-wide strip-pieced units together as shown to make block row B. Be sure the colors are placed correctly. Press all of the seams toward the left. Repeat to make a total of three rows.

Block row B.
Make 3.

7. Lay out the block rows and sashing rows as shown. Once again, be sure the colors are placed correctly. Sew the rows together and press the seams toward the block rows.

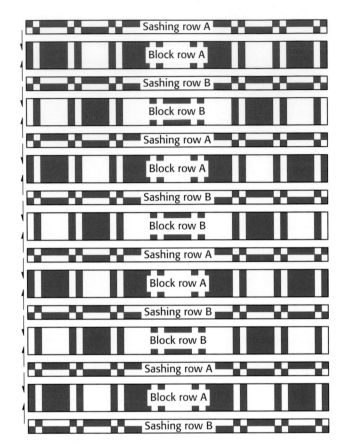

Adding the Borders

Referring to "Adding Borders" on page 90, attach the 1½"-wide dark pink inner border, the 2½"-wide light pink middle border, and the 4½"-wide dark pink outer border to the quilt top.

Finishing

Refer to "Preparing to Quilt" on page 91, "Quilting Techniques" on page 92, and "Finishing Techniques" on page 93 for detailed instructions if needed.

1. Make a backing that is 4" to 6" longer and wider than the quilt top. Cut the backing fabric into two equal lengths, remove the selvages, and sew the two pieces together along the length to make a backing with a horizontal seam. Press the seam to one side. Mark the quilt top if necessary.

2. Layer the backing, batting, and quilt top, smoothing each layer from the center outward as you go. Baste the three layers together using your preferred method. Hand or machine quilt as desired.

3. Trim the batting and backing even with the edges of the quilt top. Add a hanging sleeve if desired. Using the seven 2½"-wide pink solid strips, prepare the binding and sew it to the quilt. Make a label and attach it to your quilt.

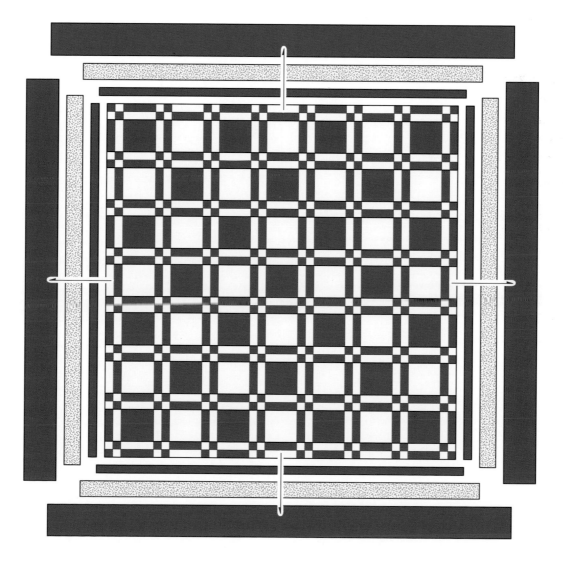

Finished Block Size: 12" x 12" (30.5 cm x 30.5 cm)
Finished Quilt Size: 67½" x 67½" (171.5 cm x 171.5 cm)

Spring Tulips

Kim Mariani used the traditional Spring Tulip block in a riot of bright 1930s prints, ranging from lollipop pinks to mint greens to sunshine yellows. This is an ideal quilt to display your collection of pretty 1930s prints.

Materials

Amounts are based on 42"-wide (107 cm) fabric.

- 13 fat quarters of 1930s prints for blocks and outer border
- 2¼ yards (2 m) of cream tone-on-tone print for blocks, setting triangles, and inner border
- 7 fat quarters of green prints for blocks and outer border
- ⅝ yard (50 cm) of green print for binding
- 4 yards (3.6 m) of backing fabric
- 72" x 72" (183 cm x 183 cm) piece of batting

Cutting

All cutting dimensions include ¼" seam allowances. Instructions are for cutting strips across the fabric width.

From the cream tone-on-tone print, cut:
- 1 strip, 18½" x 42"; crosscut into 2 squares, 18½" x 18½". Cut twice diagonally to yield 8 side triangles.
- 4 strips, 4½" x 42"; crosscut into 26 squares, 4½" x 4½"
- 8 strips, 2½" x 42"; crosscut *2 strips* into 39 squares, 2½" x 2½"
- 2 strips, 2½" x 42"; crosscut into 13 rectangles, 2½" x 4½"
- 2 squares, 9½" x 9½"; cut once diagonally to yield 4 corner triangles

From *each* of the 1930s prints, cut:
- 1 rectangle, 4½" x 8½", and 1 matching square, 4½" x 4½"
- 1 piece, 1½" x 12½"
- 2 pieces, 1½" x 11½"
- 1 piece, 1½" x 10½"
- 1 square, 2½" x 2½"

From *each* of 4 of the 1930s prints, cut:
- 1 square, 6½" x 6½"

From the remaining 1930s prints, cut a total of:
- 8 pieces, 3" x 6½"
- 100 pieces, 2½" x 6½"

From *each* of 6 of the green-print fat quarters, cut:
- 2 pieces, 2½" x 10½"
- 2 pieces, 2½" x 8½"

From the remaining green-print fat quarter, cut:
- 1 piece, 2½" x 10½"
- 1 piece, 2½" x 8½"

From the green print for binding, cut:
- 7 strips, 2½" x 42"

Making the Spring Tulip Blocks

1. To make one block, sew a 2½" cream square to a 2½" 1930s-print square; press the seam toward the print square. Sew a 2½" x 4½" cream rectangle to the unit as shown and press the seam toward the rectangle.

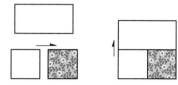

2. Draw a diagonal line on the wrong side of two 4½" cream squares. Place one cream square right sides together with a 4½" 1930s-print square and sew on the line. Trim the pair of squares ¼" beyond the seam line as shown and press the seam toward the print triangle. Place the other 4½" cream square right sides together with the 4½" x 8½" 1930s-print rectangle of the same fabric. Sew on the line, trim the fabric ¼" beyond the seam line, and press the seam toward the cream triangle.

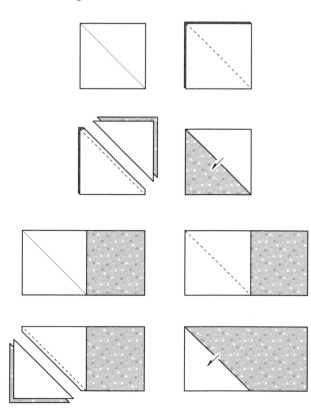

3. Sew the units from steps 1 and 2 together as shown. Press the seams toward the triangle units.

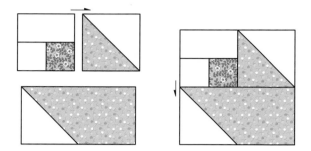

4. Draw a diagonal line on the wrong side of two 2½" cream squares. Sew one square to a 2½" x 8½" green piece and one square to a 2½" x 10½" green piece of the same fabric as in step 2. Note that the diagonal lines are going in opposite directions. Trim and press the seams toward the cream fabric.

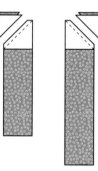

5. Sew the 8½"-long green unit to the right side of the flower unit; press the seam toward the strip. Sew the 10½"-long green unit to the bottom of the flower unit and press the seam toward the strip.

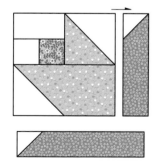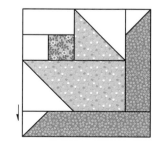

6. Sew a 10½"-long 1930s-print piece to one side of a tulip unit; press the seam toward the print piece. Turn the unit 90° counterclockwise and sew an 11½"-long 1930s-print piece to the unit; press as before. Turn the unit 90° counterclockwise again and sew another 11½"-long 1930s-print piece to the unit; press. Turn the unit counterclockwise once more and sew a 12½"-long 1930s-print piece to the unit and press.

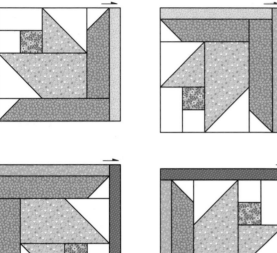

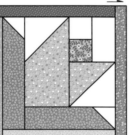

7. Repeat steps 1–6 to make a total of 13 Spring Tulip blocks.

Assembling the Quilt-Top Center

1. Lay out the blocks, side triangles, and corner triangles as shown. Sew the blocks and side triangles into rows and press the seams in opposite directions from row to row. Note that the setting triangles are oversized and will be trimmed later.

2. Sew the rows together and press the seams in either direction. Add the corner triangles and press the seams toward the corners. Trim the edges ¼" beyond the corners of each block and square up the corners.

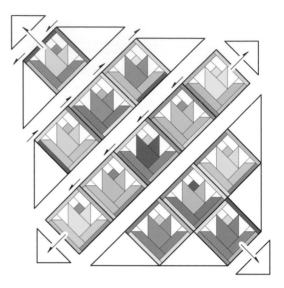

Adding the Borders

1. Referring to "Adding Borders" on page 90, attach the 2½"-wide cream border to the quilt top.

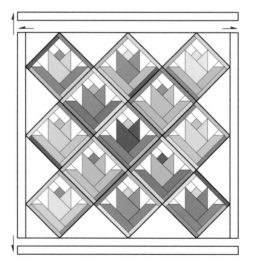

2. Make four pieced borders, each using 25 of the 2½" x 6½" 1930s-print pieces. Sew the pieces together along the length and add a 3" x 6½" 1930s-print piece to each end of all four borders as shown. Press the seams of each border in one direction.

3" x 6½"   3" x 6½"

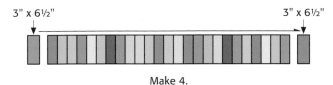

Make 4.

3. Sew two of the pieced border strips to the sides of the quilt top and press the seams toward the outer border. Sew a 6½" 1930s-print square to each end of the two remaining border strips. Sew these strips to the top and bottom of the quilt top; press the seams toward the outer border.

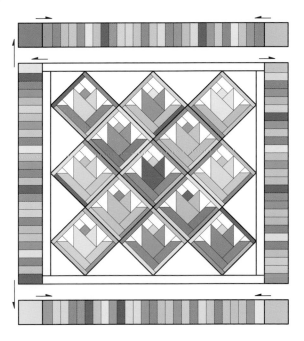

Finishing

Refer to "Preparing to Quilt" on page 91, "Quilting Techniques" on page 92, and "Finishing Techniques" on page 93 for detailed instructions if needed.

1. Make a backing that is 4" to 6" longer and wider than the quilt top. Cut the backing fabric into two equal lengths, remove the selvages, and sew the two pieces together along the length to make a backing with a horizontal seam. Press the seam to one side. Mark the quilt top if necessary.

2. Layer the backing, batting, and quilt top, smoothing each layer from the center outward as you go. Baste the three layers together using your preferred method. Hand or machine quilt as desired.

3. Trim the batting and backing even with the edges of the quilt top. Add a hanging sleeve if desired. Using the seven 2½"-wide green print strips, prepare the binding and sew it to the quilt. Make a label and attach it to your quilt.

Finished Block Size: 12" x 12" (30 cm x 30 cm)
Finished Quilt Size: 56½" x 82½" (142 cm x 208 cm)

Jam Stars

This delightfully bright quilt by Michelle Marvig features the traditional Martha Washington Star block and is a fun project that's ideal for a child's bedroom.

Materials

Amounts are based on 42"-wide (107 cm) fabric.

- 4¼ yards (3.9 m) of deep cream tone-on-tone for background
- ¼ yard (20 cm) *each* of 13 bright fabrics for blocks and pieced border
- ¾ yard (55 cm) of binding fabric
- 5 yards (4.5 m) of backing fabric
- 63" x 89" (160 cm x 226 cm) piece of batting

Cutting

All cutting dimensions include ¼" seam allowances. Instructions are for cutting strips across the fabric width.

From *each* of the 13 bright fabrics, cut*:

- 2 squares, 4¼" x 4¼"; cut twice diagonally to yield 8 quarter-square triangles
- 2 squares, 3⅞" x 3⅞"; cut once diagonally to yield 4 half-square triangles
- 8 squares, 3½" x 3½"
- 2 rectangles, 2½" x 4½"
- 4 squares, 2½" x 2½"

*Follow the diagram below to cut all of the pieces required from ¼ yard of fabric.

From the deep cream tone-on-tone, cut:

- 1 strip, 12½" x 42"; crosscut into 4 rectangles, 7" x 12½"
- 4 strips, 4½" x 42"
- 21 strips, 3½" x 42"; crosscut 14 *strips* into:
  - 52 rectangles, 3½" x 6½"
  - 52 squares, 3½" x 3½"
- 13 strips, 2½" x 42"; crosscut 7 *strips* into:
  - 26 rectangles, 2½" x 4½"
  - 52 squares, 2½" x 2½"
- 7 strips, 1½" x 42"; crosscut into:
  - 4 strips, 1½" x 38½"
  - 8 pieces, 1½" x 12½"

From the binding fabric, cut:

- 8 strips, 2½" x 42"

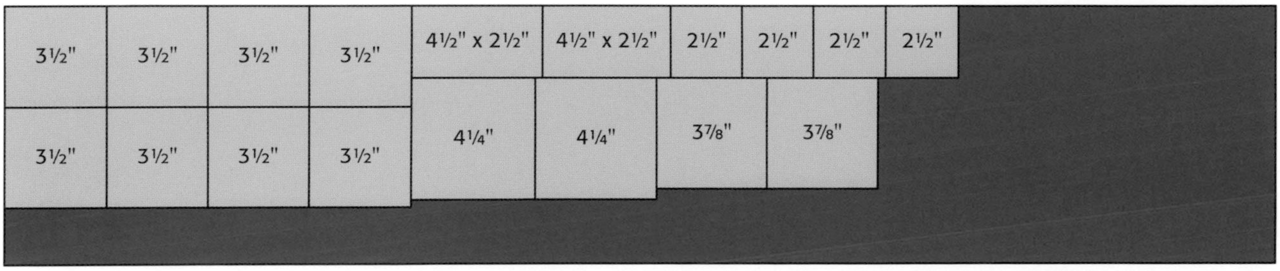

| 3½" | 3½" | 3½" | 3½" | 4½" x 2½" | 4½" x 2½" | 2½" | 2½" | 2½" | 2½" |
| 3½" | 3½" | 3½" | 3½" | 4¼" | 4¼" | 3⅞" | 3⅞" | | |

Cutting diagram for bright fabrics

Making the Martha Washington Star Block

To make the 13 blocks required, each of the bright fabrics is used in one block for the star points, in a second block for the pinwheel, and in a third block as the background for the pinwheel.

1. To make one block, select one set of eight 3½" bright squares for the star points. From another fabric of a similar color family, select one set of four 4¼" quarter-square triangles and one set of four 3⅞" half-square triangles for the background of the pinwheel. From a strong contrasting fabric, select one set of four 4¼" quarter-square triangles for the pinwheel at the center of the block. Note that the triangles cut from the 4¼" squares are smaller than those cut from the 3⅞" squares, because the larger squares are cut twice diagonally to yield triangles with the straight grain of the fabric on the long side of the triangle.

2. Sew one 4¼" background triangle to a corresponding 4¼" pinwheel triangle and press the seam toward the pinwheel fabric. Sew a 3⅞" background triangle to the pieced unit and press the seam toward the larger triangle. Make a total of four units. Arrange the units as shown and sew them together to make the pinwheel center. Press the seams as shown.

Make 4.

3. Draw a diagonal line on the wrong side of each of the eight 3½" squares chosen for the star points. Place one square, right sides together, at one end of a 3½" x 6½" cream rectangle and sew on the line. Trim the fabric ¼" beyond the seam line and press the seam toward the triangle. Sew another square on the opposite end of the rectangle as shown and trim and press as before.

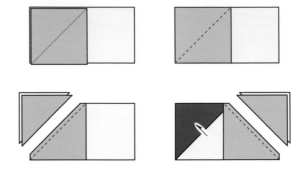

Make 4.

4. Arrange the pinwheel center, the four star-point units, and four 3½" cream squares as shown. Sew the units into rows and press the seams away from the star-point units. Sew the rows together and press the seams toward the star points.

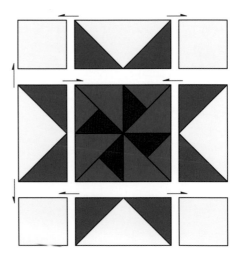

5. Repeat steps 1–4 to make a total of 13 Martha Washington Star blocks.

Assembling the Quilt-Top Center

Lay out the star blocks in five rows: three rows of three blocks alternated with two rows of two blocks. Place the 1½" x 12½" cream pieces between the blocks as shown. Place the 7" x 12½" cream rectangles at each end of the second and fourth rows and then place the 1½" x 38½" cream strips between the rows. Sew the blocks and cream pieces and rectangles together into rows and press the seams toward the cream pieces and rectangles. Sew the rows and horizontal cream strips together and press the seams toward the strips.

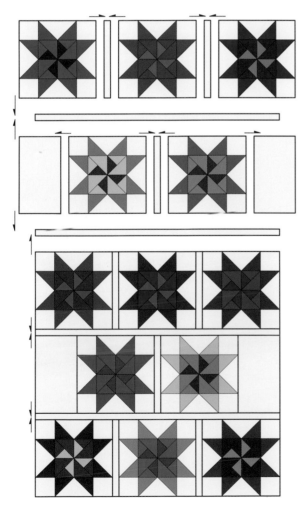

Adding the Borders

1. Referring to "Adding Borders" on page 90, attach the 2½"-wide cream border to the quilt top.

2. For the pieced border, make 26 flying-geese units, using the 2½" x 4½" cream rectangles and the 2½" bright fabric squares. Make another 26 flying-geese units, using the 2½" x 4½" bright rectangles and the 2½" cream squares. Use the method in step 3 of "Making the Martha Washington Star Blocks."

Make 26.   Make 26.

3. Sew the units in pairs of the same bright fabric to form arrow points as shown and press the seam toward the large bright triangle.

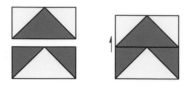

4. Sort the units into two groups of 13 arrow points, each group having one arrow point of each bright fabric. Lay out the quilt-top center and, as shown in the illustration following step 6, place five arrow-point units at the top and eight units on the right side; place five arrow-point units at the bottom and eight units on the left side. Be sure to alternate the direction of the arrows. Sew each section of arrow-point units together and press the seams of each section in one direction.

5. Measure the width of the quilt top through the center; it should be 42½" wide. The length of the top and bottom arrow sections should be 20½"; therefore, 4½" x 22½" cream strips are required to complete the top and bottom borders. Adjusting the strip length, if necessary, to fit the quilt top, trim two 4½"-wide cream strips to this length and sew these to the arrow sections as shown. Sew these borders to the top and bottom of the quilt top and press the seams away from the pieced border.

6. Measure the length of the quilt top through the center; it should be 76½" long. Cut two 4½" cream squares from the remainder of one of the 4½" strips in step 5 and sew them to the side arrow sections as shown. The length of the arrow sections should now be 36½"; therefore, 4½" x 40½" cream strips are required to complete the side borders. Adjusting the strip length, if necessary, to fit the quilt top, trim two 4½"-wide cream strips to this length (or piece them as necessary) and sew these to the arrow sections as shown. Sew these borders to the opposite sides of the quilt top and press the seams away from the pieced border.

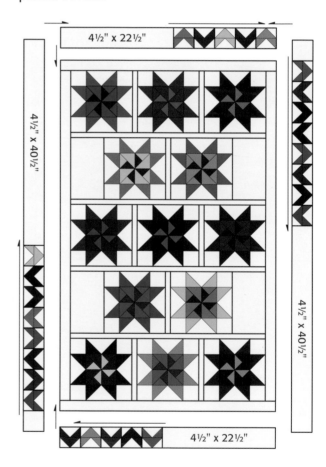

7. Referring to "Adding Borders" on page 90, attach the 3½"-wide cream border to the quilt top.

Finishing

Refer to "Preparing to Quilt" on page 91, "Quilting Techniques" on page 92, and "Finishing Techniques" on page 93 for detailed instructions if needed.

1. Make a backing that is 4" to 6" longer and wider than the quilt top. Cut the backing fabric into two equal lengths, remove the selvages, and sew the two pieces together along the length to make a backing with a vertical seam. Press the seam to one side. Mark the quilt top if necessary.

2. Layer the backing, batting, and quilt top, smoothing each layer from the center outward as you go. Baste the three layers together using your preferred method. Hand or machine quilt as desired.

3. Trim the batting and backing even with the edges of the quilt top. Add a hanging sleeve if desired. Using the eight 2½"-wide binding strips, prepare the binding and sew it to the quilt. Make a label and attach it to your quilt.

Finished Block Size: 6" x 6" (15 cm x 15 cm)
Finished Quilt Size: 63½" x 63½" (164 cm x 164 cm)

Blueberry Basket

Brilliant blues make this lovely traditional design by Chris Jurd a favorite for lovers of appliqué and quick machine piecing. This quilt is for everyone whose favorite color is blue—or red, or green, or maybe even yellow. In fact, this design would look stunning no matter what color it was made in.

Materials

Amounts are based on 42"-wide (107 cm) fabric.

- 2⅞ yards (2.6 m) of light blue print for appliqué background, Nine Patch blocks, and border
- 1½ yards (1.3 m) of blue floral for setting squares and setting triangles
- Assorted scraps of 32 blue prints for Nine Patch blocks and appliqué
- ⅝ yard (60 cm) of light blue floral for binding
- 3¾ yards (3.4 m) of backing fabric
- 67" x 67" (170 cm x 170 cm) piece of batting
- 1 yard (1 m) of fusible web (optional)
- Template plastic (optional)

Cutting

All cutting dimensions include ¼" seam allowances. Instructions are for cutting strips across the fabric width unless otherwise specified.

From the light blue print, cut *lengthwise*:
- 2 strips, 6½" x 63½"
- 2 strips, 6½" x 51½"
- 5 strips, 2½" x 65"; crosscut into 130 squares, 2½" x 2½"

From the remaining light blue print, cut:
- 2 strips, 2½" x 42"; crosscut into 30 squares, 2½" x 2½"
- 1 square, 19" x 19"

From the blue floral, cut:
- 2 strips, 9¾" x 42"; crosscut into 5 squares, 9¾" x 9¾". Cut twice diagonally to yield 20 side triangles.
- 4 strips, 6½" x 42"; crosscut into 24 squares, 6½" x 6½"
- 2 squares, 5¼" x 5¼"; cut once diagonally to yield 4 corner triangles

From *each* of the assorted blue prints, cut:
- 4 squares, 2½" x 2½" (128 squares total)

From the light blue floral, cut:
- 7 strips, 2½" x 42"

Making the Center Appliqué Block

Refer to "Appliqué Basics" on page 86 for detailed instructions.

1. Using the appliqué method of your choice, trace and cut the following pieces using the patterns on pages 36 and 37: one vase, one large petal, four medium petals, six small petals, six leaves, and three calyxes.

- For fusible appliqué, cut three ½" x 7" strips for the stems.
- If you plan to turn under the edges of your appliqués, cut three 1" x 7" strips for stems.

2. Fold the 19" light blue square once diagonally and crease gently. Place the pieces on the background square; the middle stem should be placed on the creased diagonal. When you're happy with the placement of each shape, fuse or pin them in place. Using a small blanket stitch and threads to match the appliqué fabrics, stitch the shapes in place. Trim the block to measure 18½" square.

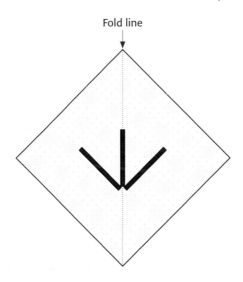

Fold line

3. Draw a diagonal line on the wrong side of four of the 6½" blue floral squares and place them right sides together on the corners of the appliqué block as shown. Sew on the drawn lines and trim the seams to ¼".

4. Press the seams toward the floral triangles.

Making the Nine Patch Blocks

Lay out five of the 2½" light blue squares and a matching set of four 2½" blue print squares in three rows of three as shown. Sew the squares together to form rows and press the seams toward the print squares. Sew the rows together and press the seams in either direction. You will make a total of 32 blocks.

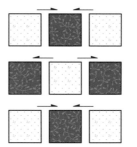 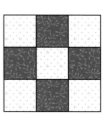

Make 32.

Assembling the Quilt-Top Center

1. Lay out the appliqué center, Nine Patch blocks, blue floral setting squares, and the side and corner triangles as shown.

2. Sew the pieces together in diagonal rows to make the four sections as shown, pressing the seams toward the blue floral fabric.

3. Sew sections 2 and 3 to opposite sides of the appliqué block, as shown, and press the seams away from the appliqué. Sew sections 1 and 4 to this center section and press the seams away from the appliqué.

Adding the Border

1. Referring to "Adding Borders" on page 90, attach the 6½"-wide light blue print border to the quilt top.

2. Using the appliqué method of your choice, trace and cut the following pieces from the patterns on pages 36 and 37: you'll need 4 calyxes, 12 medium petals, 16 small petals, 8 leaves, and 2 flower centers.

✦ For fusible appliqué, cut 4 bias strips, ½" x 13", for the stems. See "Cutting Bias Strips" on page 86 for detailed instructions.
✦ If you plan to turn under the edges of your appliqués, cut 1" x 13" bias strips for stems.

3. Using the photograph on page 32 as a guide, place the pieces on two opposite border corners. When you're happy with the placement of each shape, fuse or pin them in place. Using a small blanket stitch and threads to match the appliqué fabrics, stitch them in place.

Finishing

Refer to "Preparing to Quilt" on page 91, "Quilting Techniques" on page 92, and "Finishing Techniques" on page 93 for detailed instructions if needed.

1. Make a backing that is 4" to 6" longer and wider than the quilt top. Cut the backing fabric into two equal lengths, remove the selvages, and sew the two pieces together along the length to make a backing with a horizontal seam. Press the seam to one side. Mark the quilt top if necessary.

2. Layer the backing, batting, and quilt top, smoothing each layer from the center outward as you go. Baste the three layers together using your preferred method. Hand or machine quilt as desired.

3. Trim the batting and backing even with the edges of the quilt top. Add a hanging sleeve if desired. Using the seven 2½"-wide light blue floral strips, prepare the binding and sew it to the quilt. Make a label and attach it to your quilt.

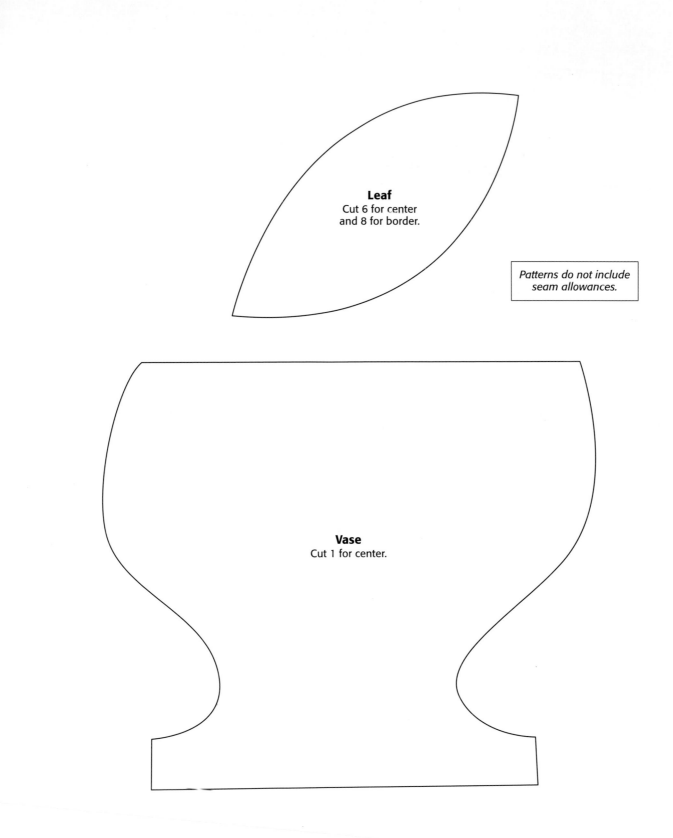

Leaf
Cut 6 for center
and 8 for border.

*Patterns do not include
seam allowances.*

Vase
Cut 1 for center.

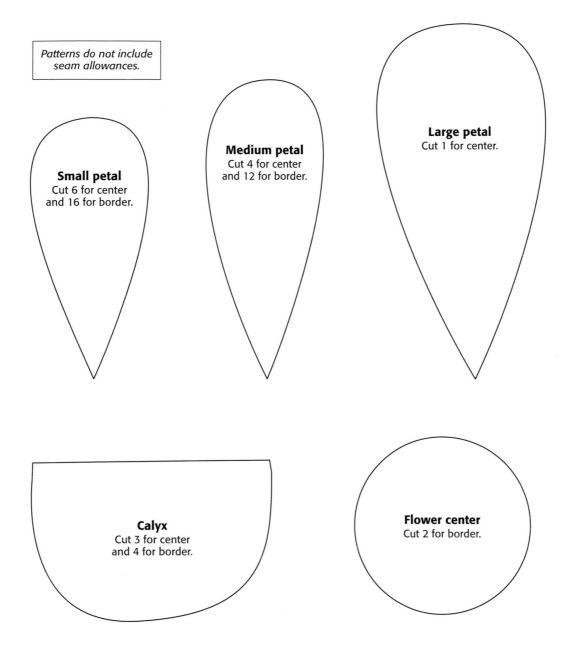

Patterns do not include
seam allowances.

Small petal
Cut 6 for center
and 16 for border.

Medium petal
Cut 4 for center
and 12 for border.

Large petal
Cut 1 for center.

Calyx
Cut 3 for center
and 4 for border.

Flower center
Cut 2 for border.

Finished Block Size: 10½" x 10½" (26.5 cm x 26.5 cm)
Finished Quilt Size: 59" x 59" (150 cm x 150 cm)

Christmas Lights

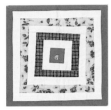

A love of the timeless Log Cabin block and the desire to make a fresh, fun quilt encouraged Linda Douglas to do a fabric swap with her friend Maree Galligan to create this Courthouse Steps design. This quilt is just made for cuddling! It would look great as a throw on a couch and is also an ideal size that can be taken anywhere.

Materials

Amounts are based on 42"-wide (107 cm) fabric.

- ¼ yard (20 cm) *each of 25 bright prints for blocks*
- 2¾ yards (2.5 m) of muslin for blocks and binding
- 1¾ yards (1.6 cm) of red print for border
- 3½ yards (3.3 m) of backing fabric
- 64" x 64" (162 cm x 162 cm) piece of batting
- Embroidery thread (optional)

Cutting

All cutting dimensions include ¼" seam allowances. Instructions are for cutting strips across the fabric width unless otherwise specified.

From *each* of 13 bright prints, cut:

- 2 pieces, 1¼" x 9½"
- 2 pieces, 1¼" x 8"
- 2 pieces, 1¼" x 6½"
- 2 pieces, 1¼" x 5"
- 2 pieces, 1¼" x 3½"
- 2 pieces, 1¼" x 2"

From *each* of the remaining 12 bright prints, cut:

- 2 pieces, 1¼" x 11"
- 2 pieces, 1¼" x 9½"
- 2 pieces, 1¼" x 8"
- 2 pieces 1¼" x 6½"
- 2 pieces, 1¼" x 5"
- 2 pieces, 1¼" x 3½"
- 1 square, 2" x 2"

From the muslin, cut:

- 7 strips, 2½" x 42"
- 1 strip, 2" x 42"; crosscut into 13 squares, 2" x 2"
- 55 strips, 1¼" x 42"; crosscut into:
  - 26 pieces, 1¼" x 11"
  - 50 pieces, 1¼" x 9½"
  - 50 pieces, 1¼" x 8"
  - 50 pieces, 1¼" x 6½"
  - 50 pieces, 1¼" x 5"
  - 50 pieces, 1¼" x 3½"
  - 24 pieces, 1¼" x 2"

From the red print, cut *lengthwise*:

- 4 strips, 3½" x length of fabric

Making the Courthouse Steps Blocks

A total of 25 blocks is required: 13 with muslin centers (block A) and 12 with print centers (block B). The completed blocks should measure 10½" square.

1. For each block A, sew 2"-long print pieces to the top and bottom of a 2" muslin square. You will press all of the seams toward the pieces you've just added. Add the 3½"-long matching print pieces to the sides of the square; press. Add 3½"-long muslin pieces to the top and bottom; press. Add 5"-long muslin pieces to the sides to complete the second round. Add the remaining four rounds in the same manner, alternating the print and muslin fabrics until there are six strips on each side of the square as shown.

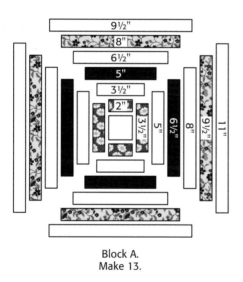

Block A.
Make 13.

2. For each block B, sew 2"-long muslin pieces to the top and bottom of a 2" print square. You will press all of the seams toward the pieces you've just added. Add 3½"-long muslin pieces to the sides of the square; press. Add 3½"-long print pieces to the top and bottom; press. Add 5"-long matching print pieces to the sides to complete the second round. Add the remaining four rounds in

the same manner, alternating the muslin and print fabrics until there are six strips on each side of the square as shown.

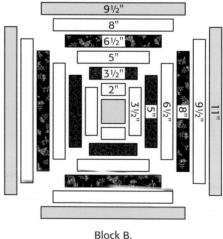

Block B.
Make 12.

Assembling the Quilt Top

1. Lay out the blocks in five rows of five blocks each. Sew the blocks into rows and press the seams in opposite directions from row to row. Sew the rows together to complete the quilt-top center. Press the seams in either direction.

2. Referring to "Adding Borders" on page 90, attach the 3½"-wide red border to the quilt top.

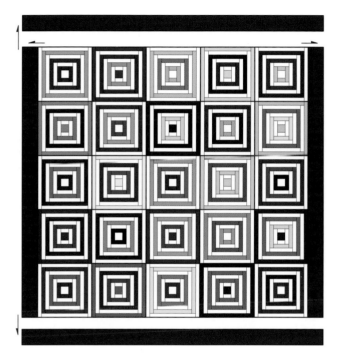

Finishing

Refer to "Preparing to Quilt" on page 91, "Quilting Techniques" on page 92, and "Finishing Techniques" on page 93 for detailed instructions if needed.

1. Make a backing that is 4" to 6" longer and wider than the quilt top. Cut the backing fabric into two equal lengths, remove the selvages, and sew the two pieces together along the length to make a backing with a horizontal seam. Press the seam to one side. Mark the quilt top if necessary.

2. Layer the backing, batting, and quilt top, smoothing each layer from the center outward as you go. Baste the three layers together using your preferred method. Hand or machine quilt as desired. This quilt was both tied with knots of embroidery thread and machine quilted.

3. Trim the batting and backing even with the edges of the quilt top. Add a hanging sleeve if desired. Using the seven 2½"-wide muslin strips, prepare the binding and sew it to the quilt. Make a label and attach it to your quilt.

Quilting and Tying Suggestion

Using three strands of embroidery floss, tie knots at the center and at each corner of the 25 blocks. Clip the threads, leaving a ½" tail. Knotted floss gives an old-fashioned look to your quilt and acts as basting for any quilting you might want to add. For minimal quilting, stitch in the ditch outside every bright-print square. If you prefer heavier quilting, outline every round of strips with stitching. Quilt a straight line or two through the border

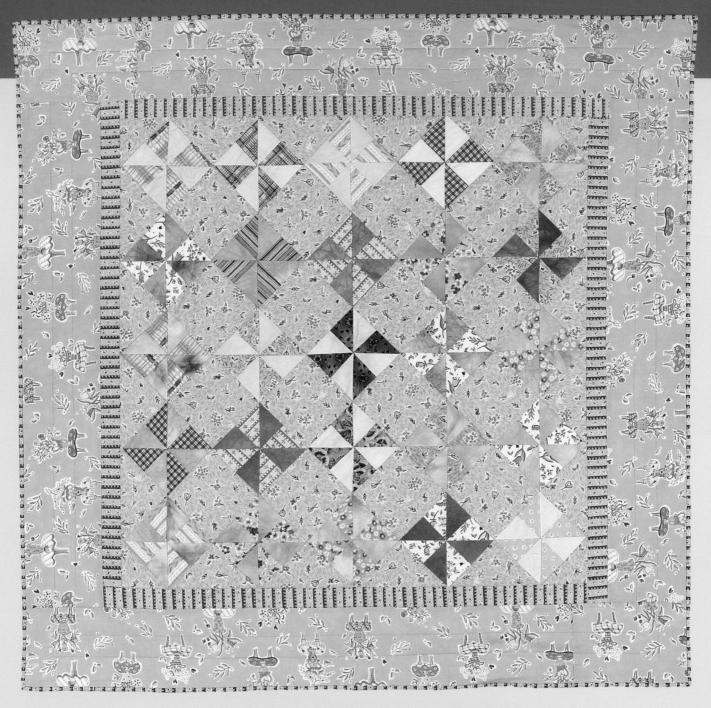

Finished Block Size: 5" x 5" (13 cm x 13 cm)
Finished Quilt Size: 51" x 51" (129.5 cm x 129.5 cm)

Sweet Dreams

In this delightful candy-colored quilt, Ruth Buchanan has created the perfect gift to bring sweet dreams to any little girl. Ruth used an enchanting border print combined with pretty scraps from her collection. To make this quilt for a boy, choose a suitable border print and match the colors in it for the quilt center.

Materials

Amounts are based on 42"-wide (107 cm) fabric.

- ◆ ¼ yard (20 cm) *each* of 8 assorted prints for blocks
- ◆ ¼ yard (20 cm) *each* of 8 light solid fabrics for blocks
- ◆ 1 yard (90 cm) of yellow print for setting squares and setting triangles
- ◆ 1 yard (90 cm) of blue print for outer border
- ◆ ¾ yard (60 cm) of yellow striped fabric for inner border and binding
- ◆ 3 yards (2.8 m) of backing fabric
- ◆ 55" x 55" (150 cm x 150 cm) piece of batting

Cutting

All cutting dimensions include ¼" seam allowances. Instructions are for cutting strips across the fabric width.

From the assorted prints, cut:

- ◆ 25 pairs of squares, 3⅜" x 3⅜" (50 squares total)

From the light solid fabrics, cut:

- ◆ 25 pairs of squares, 3⅜" x 3⅜" (50 squares total)

From the yellow print, cut:

- ◆ 1 strip, 9" x 42"; crosscut into 4 squares, 9" x 9". Cut twice diagonally to yield 16 side triangles.
- ◆ 3 strips, 5½" x 42"; crosscut into 16 squares, 5½" x 5½"
- ◆ 2 squares, 5" x 5"; cut once diagonally to yield 4 corner triangles

From the yellow striped fabric, cut:

- ◆ 6 strips, 2¼" x 42", for binding
- ◆ 4 strips, 2" x 42"

From the blue print, cut:

- ◆ 5 strips, 6½" x 42"

Making the Pinwheel Blocks

1. To make each Pinwheel block, choose one pair of the assorted print squares and a pair of light solid squares. You want contrast between the two fabrics so that the pinwheel is clearly visible. Draw a diagonal line on the wrong side of the light solid squares. Pair each solid square with a print square, right sides together, and sew ¼" from each side of the line. Cut on the line and press the seams toward the print fabric. Two squares of each fabric will yield four half-square-triangle units.

2. Sew the half-square-triangle units into two sets of two and press the seams toward the print fabric. Sew these units together to complete the block; press the seams in either direction.

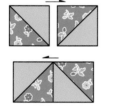
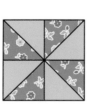

3. Repeat steps 1 and 2 to make a total of 25 Pinwheel blocks.

Assembling Quilt-Top Center

1. Lay out the blocks, 5½" setting squares, side triangles, and corner triangles as shown. Sew the blocks and side triangles into rows and press the seams toward the yellow print fabric. Note that the setting triangles are oversized and will be trimmed later.

2. Sew the rows together and press the seams in either direction. Add the corner triangles and press the seams toward the corners.

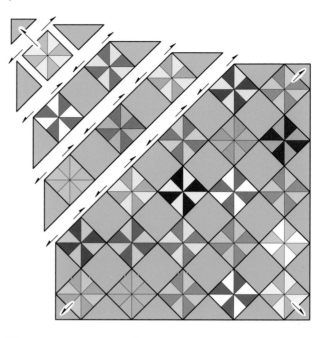

3. Trim the edges ¼" beyond the corners of each block and square up the corners.

Adding the Borders

1. The yellow striped border is applied log-cabin style. Align the raw edges of a 2"-wide yellow strip with the upper right-hand corner of the quilt top, extending the end of the strip beyond the edge as shown. Sew the border in place, stopping 6" before the bottom edge of the quilt top, and press the seam toward the border. Do not trim the end of this strip.

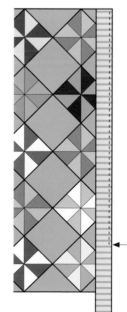

← Stop stitching 6" from bottom edge.

2. Add the next strip to the upper edge, press the seam toward the border, and trim the end of the border strip. The third strip is added to the left side in the same way. Before adding the final strip, fold the loose end of the first strip out of the way and then sew the final strip to the bottom; press and trim. Now go back and complete the stitching on the first strip, starting ½" back from where the stitching ended, and finish the seam. Press the seam toward the border strip and trim the end.

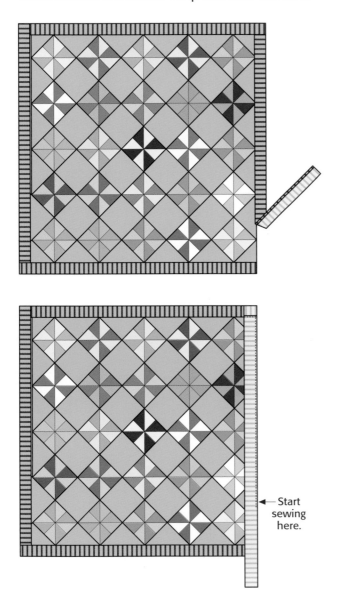

Start sewing here.

3. Referring to "Adding Borders" on page 90, attach the 6½"-wide blue print border to the quilt top.

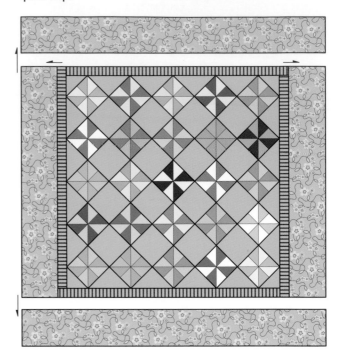

Finishing

Refer to "Preparing to Quilt" on page 91, "Quilting Techniques" on page 92, and "Finishing Techniques" on page 93 for detailed instructions if needed.

1. Make a backing that is 4" to 6" longer and wider than the quilt top. Cut the backing fabric into two equal lengths, remove the selvages, and sew the two pieces together along the length to make a backing with a horizontal seam. Press the seam to one side. Mark the quilt top if necessary.

2. Layer the backing, batting, and quilt top, smoothing each layer from the center outward as you go. Baste the three layers together using your preferred method. Hand or machine quilt as desired.

3. Trim the batting and backing even with the edges of the quilt top. Add a hanging sleeve if desired. Using the six 2¼"-wide yellow striped strips, prepare the binding and sew it to the quilt. Make a label and attach it to your quilt.

Quilting Suggestions

Finished Block Size: 7½" x 7½" (19 cm x 19 cm)
Finished Quilt Size: 58½" x 58½" (152 cm x 152 cm)

Hearts in Bloom

This charming quilt by Kerry Thomas combines fusible-web appliqué, machine piecing, and simple embroidery techniques. Kerry used scraps from her stash, not only for the Nine Patch blocks and appliqué, but also for the outer border.

Materials

Amounts are based on 42"-wide (107 cm) fabric.

- 1½ yards (1.4 m) of muslin for appliqué blocks and middle border
- 1 yard (90 cm) of pink print for inner and outer borders and binding
- Assorted scraps of dark to medium fabrics for Nine Patch blocks, appliqué, and outer border*
- Assorted scraps of light fabrics for Nine Patch blocks, appliqué, and outer border*
- 3½ yards (3.2 cm) of backing fabric
- 64" x 64" (160 cm x 160 cm) piece of batting
- ⅓ yard (30 cm) of fusible web (optional)
- Embroidery thread in green and a variety of colors
- Template plastic (optional)

The more scraps the better!

Cutting

All cutting dimensions include ¼" seam allowances. Instructions are for cutting strips across the fabric width.

From the dark to medium scraps, cut a total of:
- 65 squares, 3" x 3"

From the light scraps, cut a total of:
- 52 squares, 3" x 3"

From the muslin, cut:
- 3 strips, 8" x 42"; crosscut into 12 squares, 8" x 8"
- 5 strips, 4¾" x 42"

From the pink print, cut:
- 11 strips, 2½" x 42"
- 4 squares, 4½" x 4½"

From *all* of the assorted scraps, cut a total of:
- 80 pieces, 3" x 4½"

Making the Nine Patch Blocks

Lay out five dark to medium squares and four light squares in three rows of three as shown. Sew the squares together into rows and press the seams toward the darker squares. Sew the rows together and press the seams in one direction. You will make 13 Nine Patch blocks.

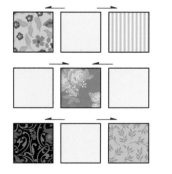

Make 13.

Making the Appliqué Blocks

Refer to "Appliqué Basics" on page 86 for detailed instructions.

1. Using the appliqué method of your choice, trace and cut the following pieces using the pattern on page 52: you'll need 12 large hearts.

2. Fold the 8" muslin squares in half and crease gently. Place each heart on a square; the heart should be centered on the fold line as shown. When you're happy with the placement of each heart, fuse or pin it in place. Stitch around the hearts, using a blanket stitch and two strands of matching embroidery thread.

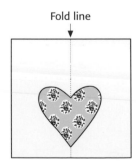

Fold line

3. Trace the embroidery design from page 52 onto the heart blocks. With two strands of green embroidery thread, use a running stitch for the stems and a detached lazy daisy stitch for the leaves. Choosing different colors for the flowers, use a backstitch or a stem stitch for the petals; use three French knots in a contrasting color for the centers.

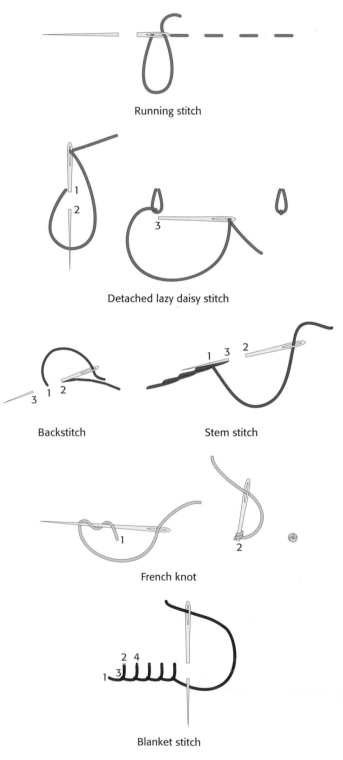

Running stitch

Detached lazy daisy stitch

Backstitch

Stem stitch

French knot

Blanket stitch

Assembling the Quilt-Top Center

Lay out the Nine Patch blocks and the appliqué blocks as shown. Sew the blocks together into rows and press the seams toward the appliqué blocks. Sew the rows together and press the seams in either direction.

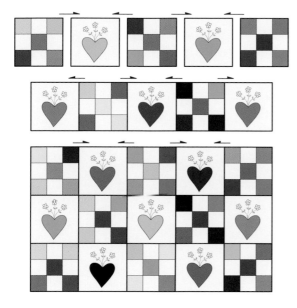

Adding the Borders

1. Referring to "Adding Borders" on page 90, attach the 2½"-wide pink print border and the 4¾"-wide muslin border to the quilt top.

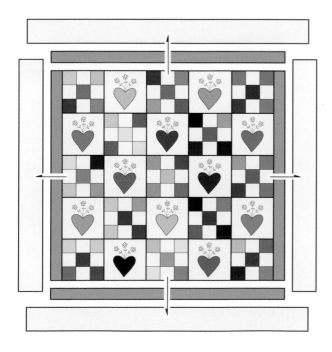

2. Enlarge the vine design on page 53 as instructed and trace it onto the corners of the muslin border, or draw the design freehand. If you use the design on page 53, you'll have nine hearts at each corner (the quilt shown on page 48 uses nine hearts at two corners and eight hearts at the other two corners). Using the appliqué method of your choice, trace and cut the following pieces using the pattern on page 52: you'll need 36 small hearts. Place the hearts along the vines as indicated on the placement diagram on page 53. When you're happy with the placement of each heart, fuse or pin it in place. Blanket-stitch around the hearts, using two strands of matching embroidery thread. Embroider the stems with a running stitch, using two strands of green embroidery thread.

3. Make four pieced borders, each using 20 of the assorted 3" x 4½" strips. Sew the strips together along the length and press the seams of each border in one direction.

Make 4.

4. Sew two of the pieced border strips to the sides of the quilt top and press the seams toward the outer border. Sew a 4½" pink print square to each end of the two remaining border strips. Sew these strips to the top and bottom of the quilt top; press the seams toward the outer border.

Finishing

Refer to "Preparing to Quilt" on page 91, "Quilting Techniques" on page 92, and "Finishing Techniques" on page 93 for detailed instructions if needed.

1. Make a backing that is 4" to 6" longer and wider than the quilt top. Cut the backing fabric into two equal lengths, remove the selvages, and sew the two pieces together along the length to make a backing with a horizontal seam. Press the seam to one side. Mark the quilt top if necessary.

2. Layer the backing, batting, and quilt top, smoothing each layer from the center outward as you go. Baste the three layers together using your preferred method. Hand or machine quilt as desired.

3. Trim the batting and backing even with the edges of the quilt top. Add a hanging sleeve if desired. Using the remaining seven 2½"-wide pink print strips, prepare the binding and sew it to the quilt. Make a label and attach it to your quilt.

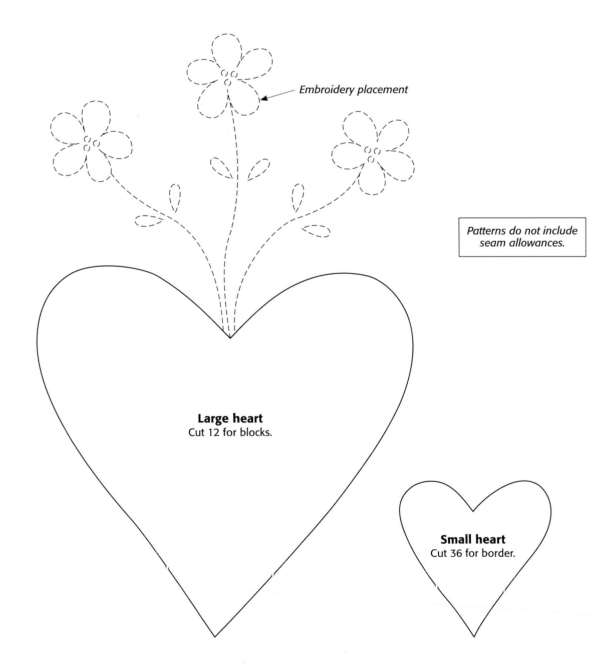

Embroidery placement

Patterns do not include seam allowances.

Large heart
Cut 12 for blocks.

Small heart
Cut 36 for border.

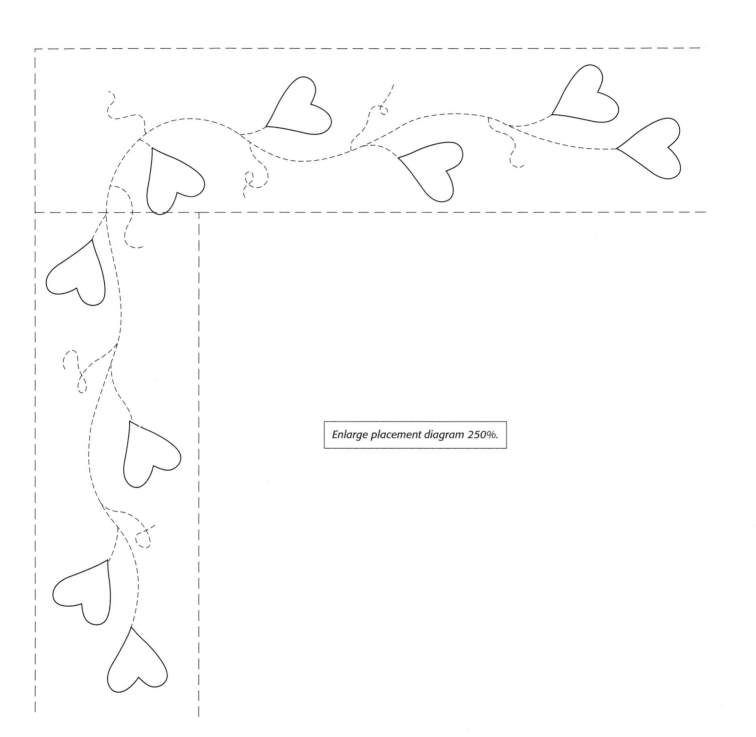

Enlarge placement diagram 250%.

Finished Quilt Size: 60½" x 60½" (154 cm x 154 cm)

Christmas Medallion

This pretty quilt by Suzy Atkins will lend a festive air to your Christmas decorating. By using Christmas colors but not Christmas motifs, Suzy's made a quilt that looks good not only at Christmas but all year round. This simple rotary-cut medallion quilt is suitable for those who want to make a quilt in a hurry.

Materials

Amounts are based on 42"-wide (107 cm) fabric.

- ✦ 8 fat quarters of red prints for Star block and borders 2, 3, and 4
- ✦ 8 fat quarters of light to medium prints for Star block and borders 3 and 4
- ✦ ¾ yard (70 cm) of green print for Star block and borders 1 and 2
- ✦ ⅝ yard (60 cm) of green striped fabric for border 1
- ✦ 2 fat quarters of green prints for borders 2 and 3
- ✦ ⅝ yard (60 cm) of red print for binding
- ✦ 3⅝ yards (3.2 m) of backing fabric
- ✦ 64" x 64" (160 cm x 160 cm) piece of batting

Cutting

All cutting dimensions include ¼" seam allowances. Instructions are for cutting strips across the fabric width.

From the light to medium prints, cut a total of:
- ✦ 20 squares, 6⅞" x 6⅞"
- ✦ 2 sets of 4 matching squares, 6½" x 6½" (8 squares total)
- ✦ 8 rectangles, 4½" x 10½"

From the red prints for the Star block and borders, cut a total of:
- ✦ 4 squares, 9¼" x 9¼"; cut twice diagonally to yield 16 quarter-square triangles
- ✦ 20 squares, 6⅞" x 6⅞"
- ✦ 8 rectangles, 4½" x 10½"

From the ¾ yard of green print for the Star block and borders 1 and 2, cut:
- ✦ 1 square, 12½" x 12½"
- ✦ 3 squares, 9¼" x 9¼"; cut twice diagonally to yield 12 quarter-square triangles
- ✦ 4 squares, 4⅞" x 4⅞"; cut once diagonally to yield 8 half-square triangles
- ✦ 4 squares, 4½" x 4½", for border 1

(Continued on page 56)

From the green striped fabric, cut:
✦ 4 strips, 4½" x 24½"

From 1 of the green-print fat quarters, cut:
✦ 4 squares, 4½" x 4½", for border 2

From the second green-print fat quarter, cut:
✦ 2 rectangles, 4½" x 10½"

From the red print for binding, cut:
✦ 7 strips, 2½" x 42"

Making the Star Block

1. Draw a diagonal line on the wrong side of eight of the 6⅞" light to medium squares. Pair each square with a 6⅞" red print square, right sides together, and sew ¼" from each side of the line. Cut on the line and press the seams toward the red fabric. You will use one half-square-triangle unit of each of the eight red prints for the star

points. Set aside the other eight half-square-triangle units for use in border 4.

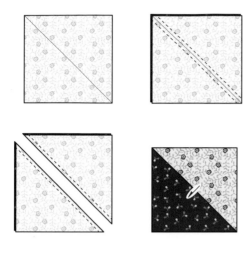

2. Lay out the 12½" green print square, the eight star-point half-square-triangle units, and one set of four of the 6½" light to medium squares as shown. Sew the units together into rows and press the seams away from the star points. Sew the rows together and press the seams away from the center. The Star block should measure 24½" square.

Adding Border 1

Sew two of the 24½"-long green striped strips to the sides of the Star block; press the seams toward the strips. Sew 4½" green squares to each end of the remaining two 24½"-long green striped strips; press the seams toward the strips. Sew these two strips to the top and bottom of the Star block and press the seams toward the strips. The quilt center should now measure 32½" square.

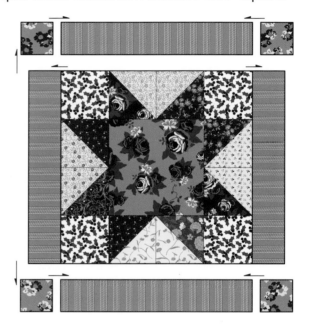

Adding Border 2

1. Sew the 9¼" red print quarter-square triangles to the 9¼" green print quarter-square triangles to make four rows as shown. Sew a 4⅞" green print half-square triangle to each end of the four rows.

Make 4.

2. Sew two of these strips to the sides of the quilt center; press the seams toward the green striped border. Be sure to place the long edge of the red triangles next to the green striped border. Sew 4½" green squares to each end of the remaining two strips; press the seams toward the squares. Sew these two strips to the top and bottom of the quilt center and press the seams toward the triangle border. The quilt center should now measure 40½" square.

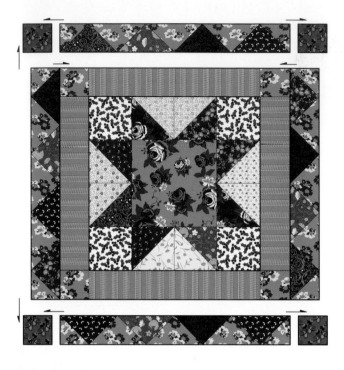

Adding Border 3

1. Randomly sew the red print, light to medium print, and green print 4½" x 10½" rectangles together as shown to make two rows of four rectangles and two rows of five rectangles. Trim 1" from each end of the five-piece rows; they should now measure 48½" long.

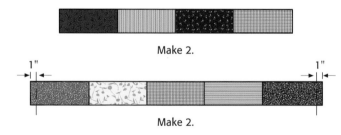

Make 2.

1" 1"

Make 2.

2. Sew the four-rectangle rows to the top and bottom of the quilt center; press the seams toward the rectangle border. Sew the five-

rectangle rows to the sides of the quilt center; press the seams toward the rectangle border. The quilt center should now measure 48½" square.

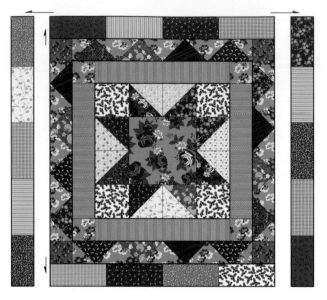

Adding Border 4

1. Draw a diagonal line on the wrong side of the remaining 12 light to medium 6⅞" squares. Pair each square with a 6⅞" red print square, right sides together, and sew ¼" from each side of the line. Cut on the line and press the seams toward the red print.

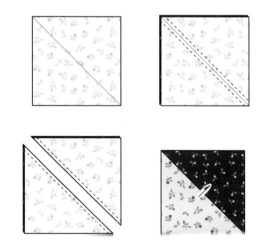

2. Using the half-square-triangle units you just made and the eight half-square-triangle units set aside in step 1 of "Making the Star Block," randomly sew them together to make four rows as shown. Be sure the red triangles are facing in the correct direction. Press the seams in one direction.

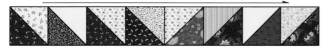

Make 4.

3. Sew two of these rows to the sides of the quilt center; press the seams toward the rectangle border. Sew the remaining set of four 6½" light to medium squares to each end of the two remaining rows; press the seams toward the squares. Sew these two rows to the top and bottom of the quilt center and press the seams toward the triangle border. The quilt top should now measure 60½" square.

Finishing

Refer to "Preparing to Quilt" on page 91, "Quilting Techniques" on page 92, and "Finishing Techniques" on page 93 for detailed instructions if needed.

1. Make a backing that is 4" to 6" longer and wider than the quilt top. Cut the backing fabric into two equal lengths, remove the selvages, and sew the two pieces together along the length to make a backing with a horizontal seam. Press the seam to one side. Mark the quilt top if necessary.

2. Layer the backing, batting, and quilt top, smoothing each layer from the center outward as you go. Baste the three layers together using your preferred method. Hand or machine quilt as desired.

3. Trim the batting and backing even with the edges of the quilt top. Add a hanging sleeve if desired. Using the seven 2½"-wide red print strips, prepare the binding and sew it to the quilt. Make a label and attach it to your quilt.

Finished Block Size: 6" x 6" (15 cm x 15 cm)
Finished Quilt Size: 60¼" x 79¾" (153 cm x 202.5 cm)

Daniel's Big Quilt

Ela Goulding made this gorgeous quilt for her four-year-old son, Daniel. This pattern is ideal if you have a collection of novelty or theme prints and want to show them off in a scrappy design. Most of the blocks are simple framed squares, but combining them with blocks made of smaller squares and double frames adds variety and movement to the quilt.

Materials

Amounts are based on 42"-wide (107 cm) fabric.

- ◆ ¼ yard (20 cm) *each* of 25 assorted novelty prints and coordinating fabrics
- ◆ 2⅛ yards (2 m) of black solid for sashing and binding
- ◆ 2⅛ yards (2 m) of yellow print for cornerstones, setting triangles, and border
- ◆ 4¾ yards (4.4 m) of backing fabric
- ◆ 66" x 86" (168 cm x 220 cm) piece of batting

Cutting

All cutting dimensions include ¼" seam allowances. Instructions are for cutting strips across the fabric width.

From the novelty prints and coordinating fabrics, cut a *total* of:

- ◆ 42 squares, 4" x 4"
- ◆ 42 strips, 1¾" x 24"
- ◆ 17 squares, 2¼" x 2¼"
- ◆ 17 strips, 1½" x 15"
- ◆ 17 strips, 1⅝" x 24"

From the black solid, cut:

- ◆ 2 strips, 6½" x 42"
- ◆ 8 strips, 4" x 42"
- ◆ 14 strips, 1⅜"; crosscut into 82 pieces, 1⅜" x 6½"

From the yellow print, cut:

- ◆ 2 strips, 9¾" x 42"; crosscut into 5 squares, 9¾" x 9¾". Cut twice diagonally to yield 20 side triangles.
- ◆ 7 strips, 6" x 42"
- ◆ 1 strip, 2½" x 42"; crosscut into 6 squares, 2½" x 2½". Cut twice diagonally to yield 24 sashing triangles.
- ◆ 2 strips, 1⅜" x 42"
- ◆ 2 squares, 5⅛" x 5⅛"; cut once diagonally to yield 4 corner triangles

Making the Framed Blocks

A total of 59 blocks is required: 42 are single-framed and 17 are double-framed blocks.

1. To make the single-framed blocks, pair the novelty print and coordinating 4" squares and 1¾"-wide strips in pleasing color combinations. Place the 4" square right sides together with the long edge of the strip, aligning the raw edges, and stitch down one side of the square. Carefully trim the strip flush with the square and press the seam toward the strip. Turn the unit 90° clockwise and sew the same strip to the next side; trim and press as before. Continue adding the strip clockwise around the square, trimming and pressing as before.

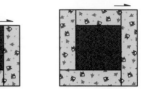

2. To make each double-framed block, use a novelty print and coordinating fabric 2¼" square, 1½"-wide strip, and 1⅝"-wide strip. Sort the squares and strips into pleasing combinations, and then sew the 1½"-wide strips to the square as in step 1. Next sew the 1⅝"-wide strip to the unit in the same way.

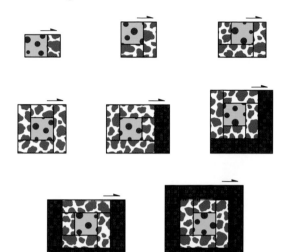

Assembling the Quilt Top

1. Sew a 6½"-wide black solid strip to a 1⅜"-wide yellow print strip along the length and press the seam toward the black fabric. Make two of these strip sets. Crosscut 58 segments, 1⅜" wide, as shown.

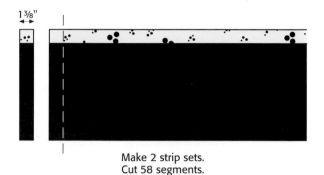

1⅜"

Make 2 strip sets.
Cut 58 segments.

2. Using the 58 sashing/cornerstone segments, 12 of the black solid 1⅜" x 6½" pieces, and the 24 yellow print sashing triangles, make 12 sashing rows as shown. Press the seams toward the black fabric.

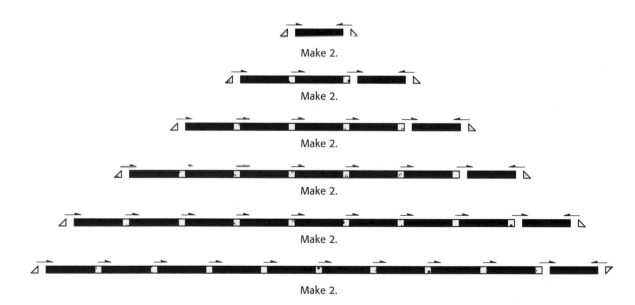

Make 2.

Make 2.

Make 2.

Make 2.

Make 2.

Make 2.

3. Lay out the blocks, the remaining 1⅜" x 6½" black strips, the sashing rows, and the yellow print side triangles as shown. Be sure to mix up the single- and double-framed blocks. Sew the blocks and black strips together into rows; press the seams toward the black strips. Sew the block and sashing rows together and press the seams toward the block rows. Add the yellow print corner triangles and press the seams toward the corners.

4. Referring to "Adding Borders" on page 90, attach the 6"-wide yellow print border to the quilt top.

Finishing

Refer to "Preparing to Quilt" on page 91, "Quilting Techniques" on page 92, and "Finishing Techniques" on page 93 for detailed instructions if needed.

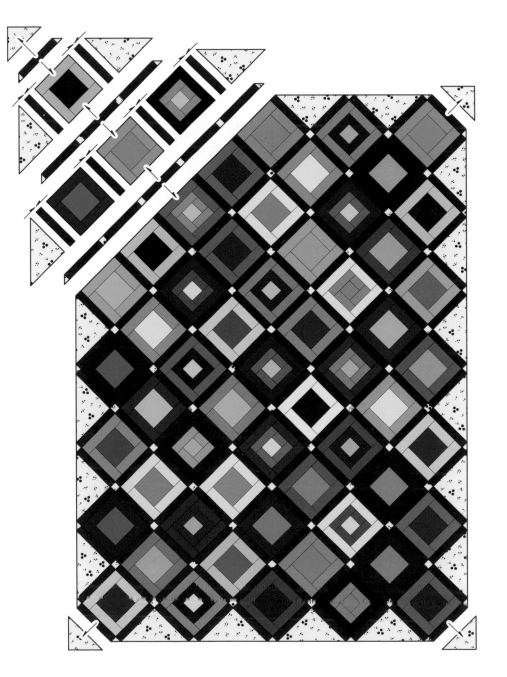

1. Make a backing that is 4" to 6" longer and wider than the quilt top. Cut the backing fabric into two equal lengths, remove the selvages, and sew the two pieces together along the length to make a backing with a vertical seam. Press the seam to one side. Mark the quilt top if necessary.

2. Layer the backing, batting, and quilt top, smoothing each layer from the center outward as you go. Baste the three layers together using your preferred method. Hand or machine quilt as desired.

3. Trim the batting and backing ½" *beyond* the quilt top to ensure a wider look to the binding. Add a hanging sleeve if desired. Using the eight 4"-wide black solid strips, prepare the binding and sew it to the quilt. Make a label and attach it to your quilt.

Quilting Suggestion

Finished Block Size: 8" x 8" (20 cm x 20 cm)
Finished Quilt Size: 57" x 45¾" (141 cm x 113 cm)

Stars and Flowers

This gorgeous country-style quilt made by Leeanne Pitman uses a variety of country-colored prints. The easily machine-pieced Star block resembles an eight-pointed star—with no set-in seams!

Materials

Amounts are based on 42"-wide (107 cm) fabric.

- ⅛ yard (10 cm) or scrap *each* of 40 assorted prints for Star blocks and appliqué
- 2¼ yards (2 m) of mottled beige fabric for block backgrounds
- ⅞ yard (80 cm) of beige star print for setting triangles
- ½ yard (50 cm) of red print for binding
- 2⅞ yards (2.6 m) of backing fabric
- 50" x 62" (127 cm x 157 cm) piece of batting
- 1 yard (90 cm) of fusible web (optional)
- Embroidery thread in green and colors to match the appliqué fabrics

Cutting

All cutting dimensions include ¼" seam allowances. Instructions are for cutting strips across the fabric width.

From the mottled beige fabric, cut:
- 3 strips, 8½" x 42"; crosscut into 12 squares, 8½" x 8½"
- 7 strips, 3" x 42"; crosscut into 80 squares, 3" x 3"
- 8 strips, 2" x 42"; crosscut into 160 squares, 2" x 2"

From *each* of the 40 assorted prints, cut:
- 2 rectangles, 2" x 4½"
- 2 rectangles, 2" x 3"

From the beige star print, cut:
- 2 strips, 12⅝" x 42"; crosscut into 4 squares, 12⅝" x 12⅝". Cut each square twice diagonally to yield 16 side triangles. (You will use only 14 triangles.)

From the red print, cut:
- 5 strips, 2½" x 42"

Making the Star Blocks

Each of the 20 Star blocks is made from two different prints, so choose the pairs of print rectangles for each block before you start sewing.

1. Draw a diagonal line on the wrong side of each of the 2" mottled beige squares. Keep your pairs of print rectangles together as you sew. Place a 2" mottled beige square, right sides together, at one end of a 2" x 3" assorted print rectangle as shown. Sew on the line, trim the seam to ¼", and press the seam toward the beige triangle. Repeat with the matching print 2" x 3" rectangle. Now repeat this step with all the 2" x 3" pairs of print rectangles.

2. Sew the 2" mottled beige squares to the 2" x 4½" pairs of assorted print rectangles in the same manner as in step 1. Note that the diagonal line is going in the opposite direction on the two rectangle sizes.

3. Sew a 2" x 3" unit from step 1 to a 3" mottled beige square and press the seam toward the square. Sew a matching 2" x 4½" unit from step 2 to this section; press the seam toward the square. Repeat this step to make two units from each print.

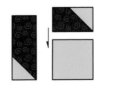

Make 2
from each print.

4. Choose two different pairs of units from step 3 to make each block. Sew the four sections together, with the same fabrics on opposite sides as shown. Make a total of 20 Star blocks.

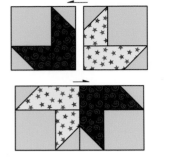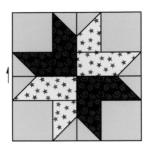

Make 20.

Making the Appliqué Blocks

1. Fold the 8½" mottled beige squares in half diagonally and gently crease. Trace the stem design from the pattern on page 71 onto the squares, aligning the center of the design along the creased line.

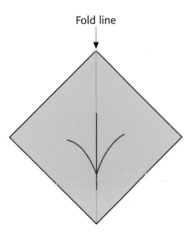

Fold line

2. Using the appliqué method of your choice, trace and cut the following pieces from the patterns on page 71: you'll need 12 of flower A, 24 of flower B, 12 of flower center A, 24 of flower center B, and 48 leaves.

3. Place the flowers at the end of each traced stem. Place flower A in the middle and flower B on either side. Add the flower centers and place the leaves along the stems. When you're happy with the placement of each shape, fuse or pin them in place. Using two strands of green embroidery thread, use a stem stitch for the stems and blanket-stitch around each of the leaves. Using two strands of embroidery thread in a color that matches each appliqué piece, blanket-stitch the flowers and their centers.

Blanket stitch

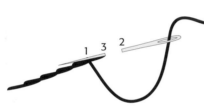

Stem stitch

Assembling the Quilt Top

1. Lay out the Star blocks, appliqué blocks, and side triangles as shown. Sew the blocks and side triangles into rows and press the seams away from the Star blocks. Note that the setting triangles are oversized and will be trimmed later.

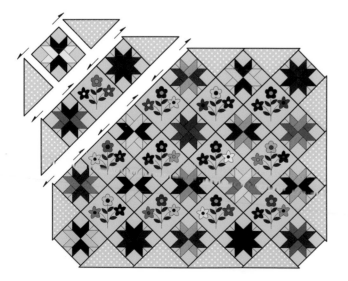

2. Sew the rows together and press the seams in either direction. Trim the edges ¼" beyond the corners of each block and square up the corners.

Finishing

Refer to "Preparing to Quilt" on page 91, "Quilting Techniques" on page 92, and "Finishing Techniques" on page 93 for detailed instructions if needed.

1. Make a backing that is 4" to 6" longer and wider than the quilt top. Cut the backing fabric into two equal lengths, remove the selvages, and sew the two pieces together along the length to make a backing with a horizontal seam. Press the seam to one side. Mark the quilt top if necessary.

2. Layer the backing, batting, and quilt top, smoothing each layer from the center outward as you go. Baste the three layers together using your preferred method. Hand or machine quilt as desired.

3. Trim the batting and backing even with the edges of the quilt top. Add a hanging sleeve if desired. Using the five 2½"-wide red print strips, prepare the binding and sew it to the quilt. Make a label and attach it to your quilt.

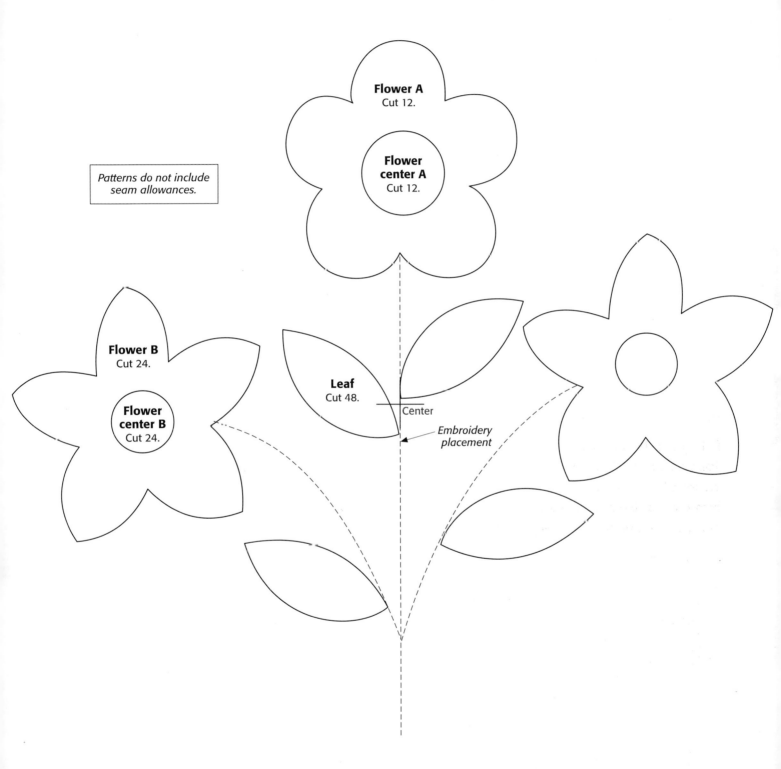

Patterns do not include seam allowances.

Flower A
Cut 12.

Flower center A
Cut 12.

Flower B
Cut 24.

Flower center B
Cut 24.

Leaf
Cut 48.

Center

Embroidery placement

Finished Block Size: 6" x 6" (15 cm x 15 cm)
Finished Quilt Size: 56" x 78½" (144 cm x 201 cm)

Turquoise Dreams

This pretty pastel quilt made by Emma Leitch has a simple block design that produces an effective secondary pattern of pink and turquoise squares set on point. Because Emma made it for her little girl, she used lots of bright, fun fabrics, but it would be just as attractive in country tones. It is a lovely, quick project that makes a much-loved and practical gift.

Materials

Amounts are based on 42"-wide (107 cm) fabric.

- 2 yards (1.8 m) of turquoise floral for blocks and outer border
- 1¼ yards (1.2 m) of mottled purple print for sashing and binding
- 1 yard (90 cm) of mottled yellow print for sashing and middle border
- ⅞ yard (80 cm) of yellow floral for blocks
- ⅞ yard (80 cm) of mottled pink print for blocks and inner border
- ⅝ yard (55 cm) of mottled turquoise print for blocks
- ½ yard (40 cm) of pink floral for blocks
- 4¾ yards (4.4 m) of backing fabric
- 62" x 84" (160 cm x 220 cm) piece of batting

Cutting

All cutting dimensions include ¼" seam allowances. Instructions are for cutting strips across the fabric width.

From the pink floral, cut:
- 2 strips, 7¼" x 42"; crosscut into 10 squares, 7¼" x 7¼"

From the turquoise floral, cut:
- 2 strips, 7¼" x 42"; crosscut into 10 squares, 7¼" x 7¼"
- 7 strips, 6½" x 42"

From the mottled turquoise print, cut:
- 5 strips, 3½" x 42"; crosscut into 48 squares, 3½" x 3½"

From the mottled pink print, cut:
- 3 strips, 3½" x 42"; crosscut into 32 squares, 3½" x 3½"
- 6 strips, 2½" x 42"

From the yellow floral, cut:
- 4 strips, 6½" x 42"; crosscut into 20 squares, 6½" x 6½"

From the mottled yellow print, cut:
- 6 strips, 1½" x 42"
- 17 strips, 1¼" x 42"; crosscut *3 strips* into:
  - 13 pieces, 1¼" x 6½"
  - 2 squares, 1¼" x 1¼"

From the mottled purple print, cut:
- 7 strips, 2½" x 42"
- 17 strips, 1¼" x 42"; crosscut *3 strips* into:
  - 13 pieces, 1¼" x 6½"
  - 2 squares, 1¼" x 1¼"

Making the Hourglass Blocks

1. Draw a diagonal line on the wrong side of each of the 7¼" pink floral squares. With right sides together, pair them with the 7¼" turquoise floral squares and sew ¼" from each side of the line. Cut the units apart on the line and press the seams toward the turquoise triangles. You will have 20 half-square-triangle units.

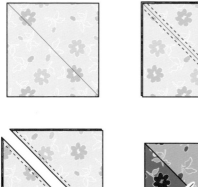

Make 20.

2. Place two of the units from step 1 right sides together, with the seams aligned, and with turquoise facing pink and vice versa. Draw a diagonal line at a right angle to the seam and sew ¼" from each side of the line. Cut the units apart and press the seams to either side. Repeat this process with all of the units from step 1 to yield 20 Hourglass blocks. These blocks should measure 6½" square.

Make 20.

Making the Square-in-a-Square Blocks

1. Draw a diagonal line on the wrong side of each of the 3½" mottled turquoise and mottled pink squares. Place a 3½" turquoise square on one corner of a 6½" yellow floral square with right sides together as shown. Sew along the line, trim the seam to ¼", and press the seam toward the triangle. Repeat this step on the three remaining corners of the yellow floral square.

2. Repeat step 1 to make a total of 12 turquoise Square-in-a-Square blocks and 8 pink Square-in-a-Square blocks. These blocks should measure 6½" square.

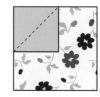

Make 12.   Make 8.

Assembling the Quilt Top

1. Sew the 1¼"-wide mottled yellow and mottled purple strips together lengthwise in pairs to make 14 strip sets; press the seams toward the purple print. Crosscut 67 segments, 6½" long, and 78 segments, 1¼" long.

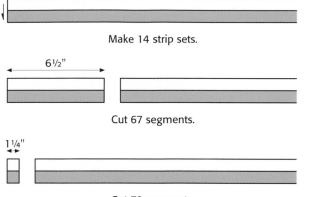

Make 14 strip sets.

6½"

Cut 67 segments.

1¼"

Cut 78 segments.

2. Set aside 22 of the 1¼"-long segments for the ends of the sashing rows and sew the remaining segments together to create 28 four-patch units.

Make 28.

3. Lay out the blocks, alternating them as shown in the quilt-assembly diagram. Place the sashing segments and four-patch units between the blocks and use the 1¼" x 6½" mottled yellow or purple pieces, 1¼"-long sashing segments, and 1¼" mottled yellow or purple squares to complete the outer edges. Note that the yellow side of the sashing segments should always be adjacent to the Hourglass blocks, and the purple side adjacent to the Square-in-a-Square blocks.

4. Sew the blocks and sashing segments together into block rows and press the seams toward the sashing. Sew the sashing segments and four-patch units together into sashing rows and press the seams toward the sashing. Sew the block rows and sashing rows together and press the seams toward the sashing strips.

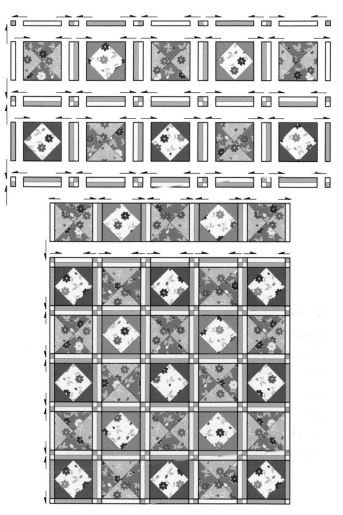

Quilt assembly diagram

5. Referring to "Adding Borders" on page 90, attach the 2½"-wide mottled pink print border, the 1½"-wide mottled yellow border, and the 6½"-wide turquoise floral border to the quilt top.

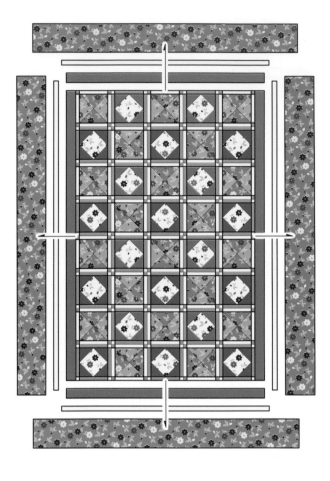

Finishing

Refer to "Preparing to Quilt" on page 91, "Quilting Techniques" on page 92, and "Finishing Techniques" on page 93 for detailed instructions if needed.

1. Make a backing that is 4" to 6" longer and wider than the quilt top. Cut the backing fabric into two equal lengths, remove the selvages, and sew the two pieces together along the length to make a backing with a vertical seam. Press the seam to one side. Mark the quilt top if necessary.

2. Layer the backing, batting, and quilt top, smoothing each layer from the center outward as you go. Baste the three layers together using your preferred method. Hand or machine quilt as desired.

3. Trim the batting and backing even with the edges of the quilt top. Add a hanging sleeve if desired. Using the seven 2½"-wide mottled purple print strips, prepare the binding and sew it to the quilt. Make a label and attach it to your quilt.

Irish Spring

Ruth Buchanan has used one of the simplest patchwork blocks, Puss in the Corner, with colors borrowed from a vintage quilt to make this calm classic. Ruth varied the fabrics in the construction to reflect the make-do ethic found in so many vintage quilts. This quilt is a wonderful opportunity to delve into your scrap box.

Materials

Amounts are based on 42"-wide (107 cm) fabric.

- ¼ yard (20 cm) *each* of 15 light to medium pink and brown fabrics for blocks
- ¼ yard (20 cm) *each* of 15 medium to dark pink and brown fabrics for blocks
- 1⅜ yards (1.3 m) of small-scale purple cherry print for side triangles
- 1⅛ yards (100 cm) of pink checked fabric for outer setting squares
- ⅝ yard (60 cm) of cream floral for inner setting squares
- ⅜ yard (35 cm) of large-scale cherry floral for corner triangles
- ⅝ yard (60 cm) of brown striped fabric for binding
- 3¾ yards (3.5 m) of backing fabric
- 66" x 76" (170 cm x 200 cm) piece of batting

Cutting

All cutting dimensions include ¼" seam allowances. Instructions are for cutting strips across the fabric width.

From *each* of the medium to dark pink and brown fabrics, cut:

- 1 square, 5½" x 5½"
- 4 rectangles, 2" x 5½"
- 4 squares, 2" x 2"

From *each* of the light to medium pink and brown fabrics, cut:

- 1 square, 5½" x 5½"
- 4 rectangles, 2" x 5½"
- 4 squares, 2" x 2"

From the cream floral, cut:

- 2 strips, 8½" x 42"; crosscut into 6 squares, 8½" x 8½"

From the pink checked fabric, cut:

- 4 strips, 8½" x 42"; crosscut into 14 squares, 8½" x 8½"

From the small-scale purple cherry print, cut:

- 5 squares, 14" x 14"; crosscut twice diagonally to yield 20 side triangles. (You will use only 18 triangles.)

From the large-scale cherry floral, cut:

- 2 squares, 8½" x 8½"; crosscut once diagonally to yield 4 corner triangles

From the brown striped fabric, cut:

- 7 strips, 2¼" x 42"

Finished Block Size: 8" x 8" (20 cm x 20 cm)
Finished Quilt Size: 60" x 70" (152 cm x 179 cm)

Making the Puss in the Corner Blocks

1. To make blocks with a dark center, you will use one 5½" square and four 2" squares, all from the same medium to dark fabric, and four 2" x 5½" rectangles from one light to medium fabric. Lay out the pieces and sew 2" x 5½" rectangles to opposite sides of the 5½" center square. Press the seams toward the rectangles. Sew a 2" corner square to each end of the remaining 2" x 5½" rectangles and press the seams toward the rectangles. Sew the top and bottom units to the center unit and press the seams away from the center. Make a total of 15 dark center blocks.

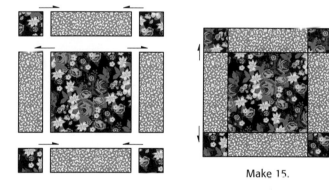

Make 15.

2. To make blocks with a light center, you will use one 5½" square and four 2" squares, all from the same light to medium fabric, and four 2" x 5½" rectangles from one medium to dark fabric. Lay out the pieces and sew them together as in step 1. Make a total of 15 light center blocks.

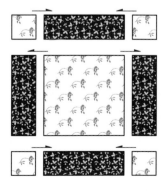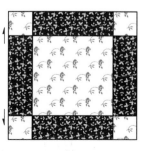

Make 15.

Assembling the Quilt Top

1. Lay out the dark and light blocks randomly, the inner and outer setting squares, the side triangles, and the corner triangles as shown. Sew the blocks and side triangles into rows. Press the seams toward the setting blocks and side triangles. Note that the setting triangles are oversized.

2. Sew the rows together and press the seams in either direction. Add the corner triangles and press the seams toward the corners.

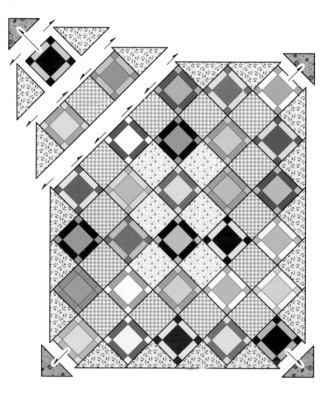

3. Leaving an equal amount of purple cherry print fabric on each side of the quilt top so the blocks will "float" on the background, trim the edges so they are straight and even, and square up the corners.

Finishing

Refer to "Preparing to Quilt" on page 91, "Quilting Techniques" on page 92, and "Finishing Techniques" on page 93 for detailed instructions if needed.

1. Make a backing that is 4" to 6" longer and wider than the quilt top. Cut the backing fabric into two equal lengths, remove the selvages, and sew the two pieces together along the length to make a backing with a horizontal seam. Press the seam to one side. Mark the quilt top if necessary.

2. Layer the backing, batting, and quilt top, smoothing each layer from the center outward as you go. Baste the three layers together using your preferred method. Hand or machine quilt as desired.

3. Trim the batting and backing even with the edges of the quilt top. Add a hanging sleeve if desired. Using the seven 2¼"-wide brown striped strips, prepare the binding and sew it to the quilt. Make a label and attach it to your quilt.

Quiltmaking Basics

Whether you're new to quiltmaking or you're simply ready to learn a new technique, you'll find this section filled with helpful information that can make putting your quilt together a pleasurable experience.

Fabrics and Supplies

Fabrics: Select high-quality, 100%-cotton fabrics. They hold their shape well and are easy to handle. Regarding fabric measurements, the term *fat quarter* refers to an 18" x 20" (45 x 50 cm) piece of fabric, and fat eighth refers to a 9" x 20" (25 x 50 cm) piece of fabric.

Freezer paper: Freezer paper is plastic coated on one side and can be ironed onto fabric without damaging it. It sticks temporarily and can be removed and reused. It is often used to help make perfectly shaped appliqué pieces, and you can find it at your local grocery store.

Fusible web: This iron-on adhesive product makes any fabric fusible. Refer to the manufacturer's directions when applying fusible web to your fabrics.

Marking tools: Various tools are available to mark fabric when tracing around templates or marking quilting designs. Use a sharp No. 2 pencil or a fine-lead mechanical pencil on lighter-colored fabrics; use a silver or chalk pencil on darker fabrics. Be sure to test your marking tool to make sure you can remove the marks easily.

Needles: A size 10/70 or 12/80 works well for machine piecing most cotton fabrics. A larger-size needle, such as a 14/90, works best for machine quilting. For hand appliqué, choose a needle that will glide easily through the edges of the appliqué pieces. Size 10 (fine) to size 12 (very fine) needles work well. For embroidery, use Sharps or embroidery needles with an eye large enough for the strands of thread, but not so large that you have difficulty pushing the needle through the fabric. For hand quilting, use Betweens, which are short, very sharp needles made specifically for this purpose.

Pins: Long, fine silk pins (with or without glass heads) slip easily through fabric, making them perfect for patchwork. Small ½"- to ¾"-long sequin pins work well for appliqué, although their shanks are thicker than silk pins.

Rotary-cutting tools: You will need a rotary cutter, a cutting mat, and a clear acrylic ruler. Rotary-cutting rulers are available in a variety of sizes; some of the most frequently used sizes include 6" x 6", 6" x 24", and 12" x 12".

Scissors: Use your best scissors only for cutting fabric. Use craft scissors to cut paper, cardboard, and template plastic. Sharp embroidery scissors or thread snips are handy for clipping threads.

Seam ripper: Use this tool to remove stitches from incorrectly sewn seams.

Sewing machine: To machine piece, you'll need a sewing machine that has a good straight stitch. You'll also need a walking foot or darning foot if you plan to machine quilt.

Template plastic: Use clear or frosted plastic (available at quilt shops) to make durable, accurate templates.

Thread: Use a good-quality, all-purpose cotton thread for piecing. For appliqué, use 100%-cotton thread or silk appliqué thread, which is widely available in most quilt shops.

Rotary Cutting

Instructions for quick-and-easy rotary cutting are provided wherever possible. All measurements include standard ¼"-wide seam allowances. If you're unfamiliar with rotary cutting, read the brief introduction below. For detailed information, see the book *The Quilter's Quick Reference Guide* by Candace Eisner Strick (Martingale & Company, 2004).

◆ Fold the fabric and match selvages, aligning the crosswise and lengthwise grains as much as possible. Place the folded edge closest to you on the cutting mat. Align a square ruler along the folded edge of the fabric. Place a long, straight ruler to the left of the square ruler, just covering the uneven raw edges of the left side of the fabric. Remove the square ruler and cut along the right edge of the long ruler, rolling the rotary cutter away from you. Discard this strip. (Reverse this procedure if you're left-handed.)

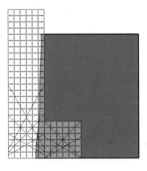

◆ To cut strips, align the newly cut edge of the fabric with the ruler markings at the required width. For example, to cut a 3"-wide strip, place the 3" ruler mark on the edge of the fabric.

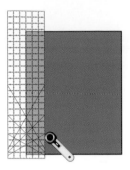

◆ To cut squares, align the left edge of the strips with the correct ruler markings. The sides of each square should have the same measurement as the width of the strips. Cut the strips into squares. Continue cutting squares until you have the number needed.

◆ To make a half-square triangle, begin by cutting a square ⅞" larger than the desired finished size of the short side of the triangle. Then cut the square once diagonally, corner to corner. Each square yields two half-square triangles. The short sides of each triangle are on the straight grain of the fabric.

¼" Finished size   ⅝"

$$\frac{1}{4}" + \frac{5}{8}" = \frac{7}{8}"$$

◆ To make a quarter-square triangle, begin by cutting a square 1¼" larger than the desired finished size of the long edge of the triangle. Then cut the square twice diagonally, corner to corner. Each square yields four quarter-square triangles. The long side of each triangle is on the straight grain of the fabric.

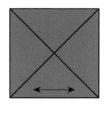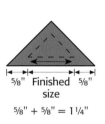

⅝" Finished ⅝"
size
⅝" + ⅝" = 1¼"

Machine Piecing

The most important thing to remember about machine piecing is that you need to maintain a consistent ¼"-wide seam allowance. Otherwise, the quilt blocks won't be the desired finished size. If that happens, the size of everything else in the quilt is affected, including alternate blocks, sashings, and borders. Measurements for all components of each quilt are based on blocks that finish accurately to the desired size plus ¼" on each edge for seam allowances.

Take the time to establish an exact ¼"-wide seam guide on your machine. Some machines have a special quilting foot that measures exactly ¼" from the center needle position to the edge of the foot. This feature allows you to use the edge of the presser foot to guide the fabric for a perfect ¼"-wide seam allowance. If your machine doesn't have such a foot, create a seam guide by placing the edge of a piece of tape, moleskin, or a magnetic seam guide ¼" away from the needle.

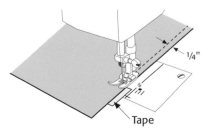

¼"

Tape

Chain Piecing

Chain piecing is an efficient system that saves time and thread. It's especially useful when you're making many identical units.

1. Sew the first pair of pieces from cut edge to cut edge, using 12 to 15 stitches per inch. At the end of the seam, stop sewing but do not cut the thread.

2. Feed the next pair of pieces under the presser foot, as close as possible to the first. Continue feeding pieces through the machine without cutting the threads in between the pairs.

3. When all the pieces are sewn, remove the chain from the machine and clip the threads between the pairs of sewn pieces.

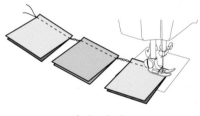

Chain piecing

Easing

If two pieces being sewn together are slightly different in size (less than ⅛"), pin the places where the two pieces should match—and in between if necessary—to distribute the excess fabric evenly. Sew the seam with the larger piece on the bottom. The feed dogs will ease the two pieces together.

Excess

Pressing

The traditional rule in quiltmaking is to press seams to one side, toward the darker color wherever possible. First press the seams flat from the wrong side of the fabric; then press the seams in the desired direction from the right side. Press carefully to avoid distorting the shapes.

When joining two seamed units, plan ahead and press the seam allowances in opposite directions as shown. This reduces bulk and makes it easier to match the seam lines. The seam allowances will butt against each other where two seams meet, making it easier to sew units with perfectly matched seam intersections.

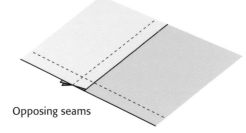

Opposing seams

Appliqué Basics

General instructions are provided here for needle-turn, freezer-paper, and fusible appliqué. Even when a specific method of appliqué is mentioned in a project, you're always free to substitute your favorite method. Just be sure to adapt the pattern pieces and project instructions as necessary.

Making Templates

To begin, you will need to make templates of the appliqué patterns. Templates made from clear plastic are more durable and accurate than those made from cardboard. And, since you can see through the plastic, it is easy to trace the patterns accurately from the book page. It's preferable to use cardboard, however, when you need to gather fabric around the template and press to form a crease.

Place template plastic over each pattern piece and trace with a fine-line permanent marker. Do not add seam allowances. Cut out the templates on the drawn lines. You need only one template for each different motif or shape. Write the pattern name and grain-line arrow (if applicable) on the template.

Cutting Bias Strips

Fabric strips cut on the bias (diagonally) are more flexible than strips cut along the straight grain. Bias strips are often used for appliqué stems, because bias-cut fabric curves easily.

To cut bias strips, align the 45° line on your ruler with a straight edge of the fabric, and cut bias strips to the width specified in the project instructions.

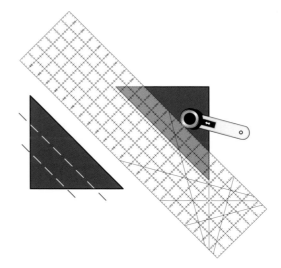

Appliquéing by Hand

In traditional hand appliqué, the seam allowances are turned under before the appliqué is stitched to the background fabric. Two traditional methods for turning under the edges are needle-turn appliqué and freezer-paper appliqué. You can use either method to turn under the raw edges. Then use the traditional appliqué stitch to attach the shapes to your background fabric.

Needle-Turn Appliqué

1. Using a plastic template, trace the design onto the right side of the appliqué fabric. Use a No. 2 pencil to mark light fabrics and a white pencil to mark dark fabrics.

2. Cut out the fabric piece, adding a scant ¼"-wide seam allowance all around the marked shape.

3. Position the appliqué piece on the background fabric. Pin or baste in place.

4. Starting on a straight edge, use the tip of the needle to gently turn under the seam allowance, about ½" at a time. Hold the turned seam allowance firmly between the thumb and first finger of one hand as you stitch the appliqué to the background fabric with your other hand. Use a longer needle—a Sharp or milliner's needle—to help you control the seam allowance and turn it under neatly. Use the traditional appliqué stitch (see page 88) to sew your appliqué pieces to the background.

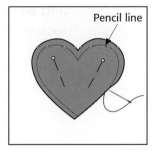

Pencil line

Freezer-Paper Appliqué

Freezer paper, which is coated on one side, is often used to help make perfectly shaped appliqués.

1. Trace around the template on the paper side (not the shiny side) of the freezer paper with a sharp pencil, or place the freezer paper, shiny side down, on top of the pattern and trace.

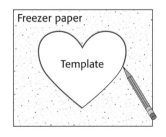

Freezer paper

Template

2. Cut out the traced design on the pencil line. Do not add seam allowances.

3. With the shiny side of the paper against the wrong side of your appliqué fabric, iron the freezer-paper cutout in place with a hot, dry iron.

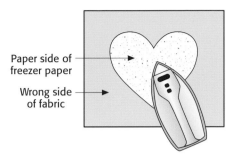

Paper side of freezer paper

Wrong side of fabric

4. Cut out the fabric shape, adding a ¼" seam allowance all around the outside edge of the freezer paper.

5. Turn and baste the seam allowance over the freezer-paper edges by hand, or use a fabric glue stick. Clip inside points and fold outside points.

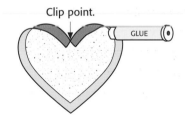

Clip point.

GLUE

6. Pin or baste the design to the background fabric or block. Appliqué the design, using the traditional appliqué stitch described on page 88.

7. Remove any basting stitches. Cut a small slit in the background fabric behind the appliqué and remove the freezer paper with tweezers. If you used a glue stick, soak the piece in warm water for a few minutes before removing the freezer paper.

Back of appliqué block

Traditional Appliqué Stitch

The traditional appliqué stitch or blind stitch is appropriate for sewing all appliqué shapes, including sharp points and curves.

1. Thread the needle with an approximately 18"-long single strand of thread in a color that closely matches the color of your appliqué. Knot the thread tail.

2. Hide the knot by slipping the needle into the seam allowance from the wrong side of the appliqué piece, bringing it out on the fold line.

3. Work from right to left if you're right-handed or from left to right if you're left-handed.

4. To make the first stitch, insert the needle into the background right next to where the needle came out of the appliqué fabric. Bring the needle up through the edge of the appliqué, about ⅛" from the first stitch.

5. As you bring the needle up, pierce the basted edge of the appliqué piece, catching only one or two threads of the edge.

6. Again, take a stitch into the background block right next to where the thread came up through the appliqué. Bring the needle up about ⅛" from the previous stitch, again catching the basted edge of the appliqué.

7. Give the thread a slight tug and continue stitching.

Note: The stitches in the appliqué illustration are enlarged to show placement. The stitches should not show in the completed work.

Appliqué stitch

8. To end your stitching, pull the needle through to the wrong side. Behind the appliqué piece, take two small stitches, making knots by taking your needle through the loops. Check the right side to see if the thread shows through the background. If it does, take one more small stitch on the back side to direct the tail of the thread under the appliqué fabric.

Fusible Appliqué

Using fusible web is a fast and fun way to appliqué. If the appliqué pattern is asymmetrical, you need to make a reverse tracing of the pattern so the pattern will match the original design when fused in place. Otherwise, your finished project will be the reverse of the project shown in the book. You don't need to make reverse tracings for patterns that are symmetrical or for ones that are already printed in reverse. Refer to the manufacturer's directions when applying fusible web to your fabrics; each brand is a little different, and pressing it too long may result in fusible web that doesn't stick well.

1. Trace or draw the shape on the paper-backing side of the fusible web. Cut out the shape, leaving about a ¼" margin all around the outline.

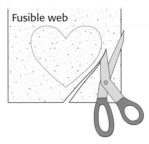

Fusible web

2. Fuse the shape to the wrong side of your fabric.

Wrong side of fabric

3. Cut out the shape exactly on the marked line.

4. Remove the paper backing, position the shape on the background, and press it in place with your iron.

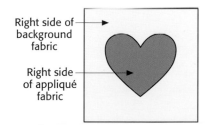

Right side of background fabric

Right side of appliqué fabric

Assembling the Quilt Top

From squaring up your blocks—to make them easier to sew together—to adding borders that aren't wavy, you'll find all you need to know about assembling your quilt top here.

Squaring Up Blocks

When your blocks are complete, take the time to square them up. Use a large, square ruler to measure your blocks and make sure they are the desired size plus an exact ¼" on each side for seam allowances. For example, if you're making

9" blocks, they should all measure 9½" before you sew them together. Trim the larger blocks to match the size of the smallest one. Be sure to trim all four sides; otherwise, your block will be lopsided.

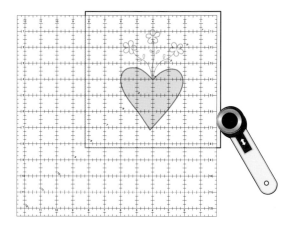

If your blocks are not the required finished size, adjust all the other components of the quilt, such as sashing and borders, accordingly.

Making Straight-Set Quilts

1. Arrange the blocks as shown in the assembly diagram included with the project instructions.

2. Sew the blocks together in horizontal rows, pressing the seams in opposite directions from one row to the next, unless directed otherwise in the project instructions.

3. Sew the rows together, making sure to match the seams between the blocks.

Making Diagonal-Set Quilts

1. Lay out the pieced blocks, alternate blocks (if any), side triangles, and corner triangles according to the assembly diagram.

2. Sew the blocks and side triangles into diagonal rows. Press as directed in the project instructions or diagram.

3. Sew the rows together, matching all the seam intersections; press as directed.

4. Sew a corner triangle to each of the four corners. Press the seams toward the corners.

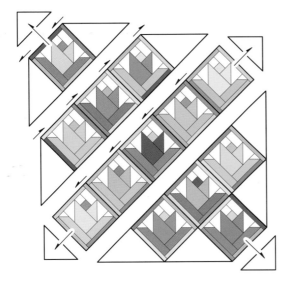

5. Use a long ruler to trim all four sides of the quilt top. Align the ¼" measurement line on the ruler with two block points at the edge of the quilt top and trim, leaving exactly ¼" for seam allowances. Use the end of your long ruler or a square ruler to square up the four corners.

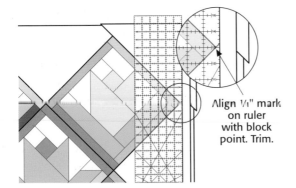

Align ¼" mark on ruler with block point. Trim.

Adding Borders

For best results, do not cut border strips and sew them directly to the quilt without measuring first. The edges of a quilt often measure slightly longer than the distance through the quilt center, due to stretching during construction. Instead, measure the quilt top through the center in both directions to determine how long to cut the border strips. This step ensures that the finished quilt will be as straight and as "square" as possible, without wavy edges.

Many of the quilts in this book call for plain border strips. Some of these strips are cut along the crosswise grain and seamed where extra length is needed. Others are cut along the length of the fabric and do not need to be pieced.

1. Measure the length of the quilt top through the center. Determine the midpoints of the border and quilt top by folding them in half and creasing or pinning the centers. Then pin the borders to opposite sides of the quilt top, matching the center marks and ends and easing as necessary. Sew the border strips in place. Press the seams toward the borders.

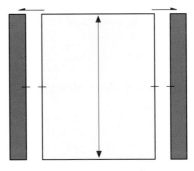

Measure center of quilt, top to bottom. Mark centers.

2. Measure the width of the quilt top through the center, including the side borders just added. Mark the centers of the quilt edges and the border strips. Pin the borders to the top and bottom edges of the quilt top, matching the center marks and ends and easing as necessary. Sew the border strips in place. Press the seams toward the border.

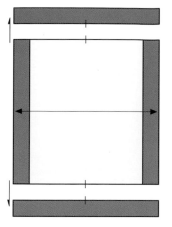

Measure center of quilt, side to side, including border strips. Mark centers.

Preparing to Quilt

If you'll be quilting your project by hand or on your home sewing machine, you'll want to follow the directions below for marking, layering, basting, and quilting. However, if you plan to have a professional machine quilter quilt your project, check with that person before preparing your finished quilt top in any way. Quilts do not need to be layered and basted for long-arm machine quilting, nor do they usually need to be marked.

Marking the Quilting Lines

Whether you mark quilting designs on the quilt top or not depends upon the type of quilting you will be doing. Marking isn't necessary if you plan to quilt in the ditch (along the seam lines) or outline quilt a uniform distance from seam lines. For more complex quilting designs, however, mark the quilt top before the quilt is layered with batting and backing. Choose a marking tool that will be visible on your fabric and test it on fabric scraps to be sure the marks can be removed easily. See "Marking tools" on page 83 for options. Masking tape can be used to mark straight quilting lines. Tape only small sections at a time

and remove the tape when you stop at the end of the day, or the sticky residue may be difficult to remove from the fabric.

Layering and Basting the Quilt

Once you complete the quilt top and mark it for quilting, assemble the quilt "sandwich," which consists of the backing, batting, and quilt top. The quilt backing and batting should be about 4" to 6" longer and wider than the quilt top. Batting comes packaged in standard bed sizes, or it can be purchased by the yard.

For large quilts, you may need to sew two or three lengths of fabric together to make a backing. Trim away the selvages before piecing the lengths together. Press the seams to one side.

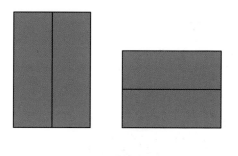

1. Spread the backing, wrong side up, on a flat, clean surface. Anchor it with pins or masking tape. Be careful not to stretch the backing out of shape.

2. Spread the batting over the backing, smoothing out any wrinkles.

3. Center the pressed quilt top, right side up, on top of the batting. Smooth out any wrinkles and make sure the quilt-top edges are parallel to the edges of the backing.

4. For hand quilting, baste with needle and thread, starting in the center and working diagonally to each corner. Then baste a grid of horizontal and vertical lines 6" to 8" apart. Finish by basting around the edges. For machine quilting, baste the layers with No. 2 rustproof safety pins. Place pins about 6" to 8" apart, away from the areas you intend to quilt.

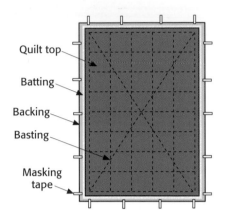

Quilt top

Batting

Backing

Basting

Masking
tape

Quilting Techniques

Some of the projects in this book were hand quilted, others were machine quilted, and some were quilted on long-arm quilting machines. The choice is yours!

Hand Quilting

To quilt by hand, you will need short, sturdy needles (called Betweens), quilting thread, and a thimble to fit the middle finger of your sewing hand. Most quilters also use a frame or hoop to support their work. Use the smallest needle you can comfortably handle; the finer the needle, the smaller your stitches will be. The basics of hand quilting are explained below. For more information on hand quilting, refer to *Loving Stitches: A Guide to Fine Hand Quilting, Revised Edition,* by Jeana Kimball (Martingale & Company, 2003).

1. Thread your needle with a single strand of quilting thread about 10" long. Make a small knot and insert the needle in the top layer about 1" from the place where you want to start stitching.

Pull the needle out at the point where quilting will begin and gently pull the thread until the knot pops through the fabric and into the batting.

2. Take small, evenly spaced stitches through all three quilt layers. Rock the needle up and down through all layers until you have three or four stitches on the needle. Place your other hand underneath the quilt so you can feel the needle point with the tip of your finger when a stitch is taken.

3. To end a line of quilting, make a small knot close to the last stitch; then backstitch, running the thread a needle's length through the batting. Gently pull the thread until the knot pops into the batting; clip the thread at the quilt's surface.

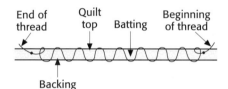

End of
thread

Quilt
top

Batting

Beginning
of thread

Backing

Machine Quilting

Machine quilting is suitable for all types of quilts, from wall hangings to crib quilts to full-size bed quilts. Marking the quilting design is only necessary if you need to follow a grid or a complex pattern. It isn't necessary if you plan to quilt in the ditch, outline quilt a uniform distance from seam lines, or free-motion quilt in a random pattern.

For straight-line quilting, it is extremely helpful to have a walking foot to help feed the quilt layers through the machine without shifting or puckering. Some machines have a built-in walking foot; other machines require a separate attachment.

For free-motion quilting, you need a darning foot and the ability to drop or cover the feed dogs on your machine. With this type of quilting, you guide the fabric in the direction of the design rather than turning the fabric under the needle.

Use free-motion quilting to outline quilt a fabric motif or to create stippling or other curved designs.

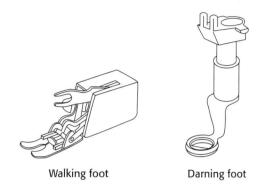

Walking foot   Darning foot

Long-Arm Machine Quilting

If you prefer to have your quilt quilted by a professional, ask at your local quilt shop for references about someone in your area who does this type of work. Generally, for long-arm quilting, you don't layer and baste the quilt prior to giving it to the quilter, nor do you have to mark the quilting designs. Check with your long-arm professional to be sure of specifications regarding batting and backing sizes before cutting or piecing yours.

Finishing Techniques

Bind your quilt, add a hanging sleeve if one is needed, label your quilt, and you're finished!

Cutting Straight-Grain Binding

For a double-fold binding, cut strips 2" to 2½" wide across the width of the fabric. (Some quilters prefer narrow binding, especially if a low-loft batting is used. If you're using a thicker batting, you may want to use 2½"-wide strips.) You will need enough strips to go around the perimeter of the quilt, plus 10" for seams and to turn the corners.

Attaching the Binding

1. Sew the binding strips together to make one long strip. Trim excess fabric and press the seams open to make one long piece of binding.

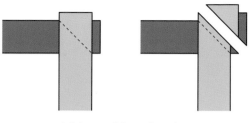

Joining straight-grain strips

2. Fold the strip in half lengthwise, wrong sides together, and press.

3. Trim the batting and backing even with the quilt top. If you plan to add a hanging sleeve, do so now before attaching the binding (see page 95).

4. Starting near the middle of one side of the quilt, align the raw edges of the binding with the raw edges of the quilt top. Using a walking foot and a ¼"-wide seam allowance, begin stitching the binding to the quilt, leaving a 6" tail unstitched. Stop stitching ¼" from the corner of the quilt.

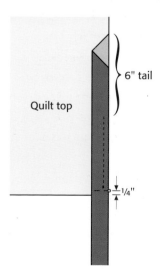

6" tail

Quilt top

¼"

5. Lift the needle out of the quilt; then turn the quilt so you will be stitching down the next side. Fold the binding up, away from the quilt, with raw edges aligned. Fold the binding back down onto itself, even with the edge of the quilt top. Begin stitching ¼" from the corner, backstitching to secure the stitches. Repeat the process on the remaining edges and corners of the quilt.

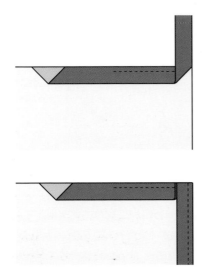

6. On the last side of the quilt; stop stitching about 7" from where you began. Overlap the ending binding tail with the starting tail. Trim the binding ends with a perpendicular cut so the overlap is exactly the same distance as the cut width of your binding strips. (If your binding strips are 2½" wide, the overlap should be 2½"; for 2"-wide binding, the overlap should be 2".)

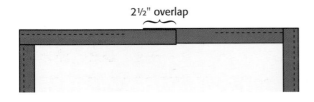

2½" overlap

7. Open up the two ends of the folded binding. Place the tails right sides together so they join to form a right angle as shown. Pin the binding tails together, then mark a diagonal stitching line from corner to corner.

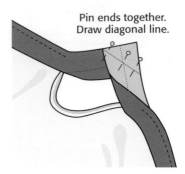

Pin ends together.
Draw diagonal line.

8. Stitch the binding tails together on the marked line. Trim the seam allowance to ¼"; press the seam open to reduce bulk. Refold the binding, align the edges with the raw edges of the quilt top, and finish sewing the binding in place.

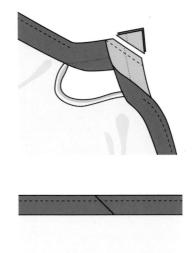

9. Fold the binding to the back of the quilt top to cover the machine stitching line. Hand stitch the binding in place, mitering the corners.

Quilt back

Adding a Hanging Sleeve

If you plan to display your finished quilt on the wall, be sure to add a hanging sleeve to hold the rod.

1. Using leftover fabric from the quilt backing, cut a strip 6" to 8" wide and 1" shorter than the width of your quilt. Fold the short ends under ½", then again ½" to make a hem. Stitch in place.

2. Fold the fabric strip in half lengthwise, wrong sides together, and baste the raw edges to the top of the quilt back. The top edge of the sleeve will be secured when the binding is sewn on the quilt.

3. After the binding has been attached, finish the sleeve by blindstitching the bottom of the sleeve in place. Push the bottom edge of the sleeve up just a bit to provide a little give so the hanging rod does not put strain on the quilt.

Signing Your Quilt

Future generations will be interested to know more than just who made the quilt and when, so be sure to include the name of the quilt, your name, your hometown and state, the date, the name of the recipient if the quilt is a gift, and any other interesting or important background about the quilt. The information can be handwritten, typed, or embroidered.

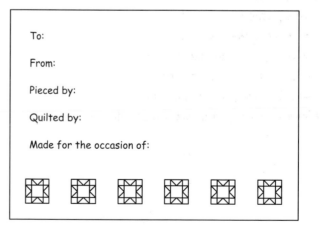